To John & Jean

to give you memories of
good beer
          Fred & Judy Clarke
              AUGUST 1978

Pubs and Pub Signs

A Colourmaster Publication

Colourmaster International (Photo Precision Limited)
Caxton Road St. Ives Huntingdon England

Acknowledgements

The publishers express their gratitude to the
following individuals and organisations:–
The Brewers' Society and Whitbread & Company
Ltd. for permission to reproduce illustrations
of pub signs. Watney Mann Ltd. for
photographs of some of their houses.
Mrs. Margaret Mainprize for permission to
include the illustration of the Three Mariners.
Helpful factual information has been supplied
by Trust Houses Forte Ltd., Bass Charrington
Ltd., Mr. R. J. Webber, Mr. J. W. Gregory and
Mr. N. R. Draycott.

ISBN 0 85933 105 9

Published by Colourmaster International (Photo Precision Limited)
Caxton Road St. Ives Huntingdon England

Some readers may be surprised to learn that ale was being brewed here before the Romans landed and that ale houses were trading before the Normans came. The pub has a long and proud tradition. A unique and seemingly indestructible British institution, it is the envy of the rest of the world.

Among our 70,000 licensed premises there are some that are set in dismal surroundings and are nondescript in themselves but there are also many of outstanding architectural interest and importance, located in some of the most beautiful parts of Britain. Some of them have fascinating links with Church and State while others have associations with famous and also with infamous figures from many walks of life—artists and men of letters, highwaymen and smugglers, cranks and criminals, some of them notable, others notorious, all of them interesting.

Our pubs are an integral part of the British way of life and the ensuing pages are designed to provide an interesting illustrated background to the story and to say something about the origins of the signs which nearly all of them continue to carry.

Pubs

No one can say when or where the first pub
was founded but we had mastered the art of
brewing ale long before the Romans arrived
on our shores.

The ingredients consisted of malt, which was
made mainly from barley, water and yeast
and it was not until as late as the fifteenth
century that an improved beverage, later to
become beer, was perfected by the
introduction of hops. Referring to ale, the
Roman historian Pliny the Elder, was able
to moralise about the whole world being
*'addicted to drunkenness; the perverted
ingenuity of man has given even to water the
power of intoxicating where wine is not
procurable. Western nations intoxicate
themselves by means of moistened grain'*.

Five hundred years later and after the
influences of Christianity had reached
Northern Europe, Saint David was busily
proselytizing and founding monasteries in
Wales. He was obviously concerned about
the drinking habits of the local populace and
felt inspired enough to decree: *'Those who
get drunk through ignorance must do penance
fifteen days, if through negligence forty days,
if through contempt, three quarantains'*.

It would appear that the situation worsened
and by the year 695 we hear of the King of
Kent ordering that if any priest *'is too drunk
to discharge his duty, he shall abstain from his
ministrations, pending a decision from the
bishop'*.

During the years leading up to the Norman
invasion there appear to have been a
number of ale-houses in existence in most
towns, villages and even alongside some of
the old Roman roads, which by now had

In the ancient ecclesiastical town of Dorchester (Oxon), the Guest House, used to accommodate pilgrims and travellers, is the only part of the monastic buildings to have escaped demolition in the 16th century. The nearby inn, The George, was originally a brew-house used by monks at the Abbey.

probably fallen into considerable neglect and disrepair. The publican lived close to the ale hut and he was, of course, also the brewer.

Travellers were able to identify ale-houses by the long wooden poles which had been adapted from the Romans, who had long ago used various trade signs. Archaeologists have excavated a number of these early emblems from the ruins of Pompeii and Herculaneum. Some of the early ale-houses also sold wine and an evergreen hanging outside the building was used to denote this.

It must come as no surprise to hear of the strong arm of the law taking an interest in the spread of these drinking establishments and under the rule of King Edgar (959-75) it was decreed that each village should only be allowed one ale-house. No doubt a number of ale-houses were forced to close because of this measure and a new innovation aimed at curbing drunkenness required the fitting of pegs at regular intervals inside drinking horns and prohibiting the drinker from going beyond a fresh mark at each draught. However, this well intentioned idea failed to make any drastic improvement and in fact actually encouraged competitive drinking bouts. In 1102 it was ruled that priests should not indulge in 'drinking to pegs' and it is said that the expression of 'taking someone down a peg' had its origins here.

The Church was also taking restrictive measures against the misuse of alcohol and various ecclesiastical canons were issued. *'Let no priest drink at taverns as secular people do. Nor ought men to drink or eat intemperately . . . and drink to madness* their legal and economic status as one of subjection, so that they could make it as a "strange" witness of unbelief. With one hand, the church would seek to protect Jews; with the other, it would oppress them.

Jews are *suited only for slaughter*. In the ancient church, the most overblown outcry of antagonism against Jews was that of John Chrysostom (ca. 344-407). Nicknamed "the golden-mouthed" because of his oratorical gifts, he became "poison-mouthed" in a series of eight sermons "against the Jews" preached at Antioch, where he was bishop, beginning in 386.

The first sermon discloses what concerned Chrysostom. As he preached it, "the festivals of the wretched and miserable Jews . . . are about to take place. And many who belong to us . . . attend their festivals. It is this evil practice I now wish to drive from the church" (Chrysostom: 86). Some Christians and Jews were friendly and visited in each other's homes. To stop this, Chrysostom attacked Judaism and the synagogue, proclaiming that the Jews had thrown away all the good things they had received from God, turning their backs on the light to sit in darkness. But we gentiles, having been in the dark, welcomed the light when it appeared. Further, they crucified the One whom we worship. "This is why they are wretched, because when others embraced and welcomed the good things given to them, the Jews refused them" (Chrysostom: 87).

Chrysostom fell to a new low in talking of Jews as "dogs, . . . wild animals . . . suited only for slaughter" (Chrysostom: 89). He declared that the synagogue "is not only a house of prostitution and a theater, it is also a hideout for thieves and a den of wild animals." It is a home of demons in which "no Jew worships God," certainly not in "a temple of idolatry" (Chrysostom: 90).

These images of Jews and Judaism moved well beyond the bounds of rhetoric. Ambrose instructed the emperor on how Jews were to be treated, and Augustine's views became the guidelines of medieval practice. It is not difficult to imagine how a preacher giving vent to views like Chrysostom's could inspire an outbreak of mob violence. Policies of the state toward Jews are now inspired by anti-Jewish images.

Jews *may not live among us*. Lest readers gain the mistaken impression that Christian anti-Judaism is not a problem for Protestants, because it arose prior to and was no doubt overcome by

59

the Reformation, we take one last look at anti-Jewish images and practices. Early in his activity as a reformer, Martin Luther knew of and felt badly about how Jews had been treated in Christian history. To address this problem he wrote a book called *That Jesus Christ Was Born A Jew* (1523), noting that Christians have "so treated the Jews that to be a good Christian one would have to become a Jew" (Luther: 33). The fly in Luther's ointment was his expectation that, if Jews were treated better and instructed in the gospel, "many of them will become real Christians." We can "expect them to come over to us" (Luther: 34).

Luther's tract gives evidence that some Jews did convert, but his hopes failed to materialize. Jews seized upon their new freedom, argued with Luther, and drew some Christians toward the synagogue. As an old man, chronically ill and capable of a venomous attitude, Luther turned on the Jews. In a tract written in 1543, three years before his death, he asked: "What then shall we Christians do with this damned, rejected race of Jews?" (Luther: 34).

His "honest advice" consisted of eight points: (1) their synagogues should be set on fire; (2) their homes should be destroyed; (3) their prayer books and Talmuds should be taken from them; (4) their rabbis should be prohibited from teaching under threat of death; (5) they should be denied passport and traveling rights; (6) they should be prevented from lending money at interest (one of the few forms of business permitted to Jews); (7) they should be put to work at manual labor; and (8) if necessary they should be expelled from the country (Luther: 35-36). Thus will we "be free of this insufferable devilish burden—the Jews" (Luther: 36). The Nazis would reprint Luther's tracts against the Jews and cite them in their defense at the Nuremberg trials (Hilberg: 689-690).

Luther's last sermon pleaded that all Jews be expelled from Saxony. He was not unaware that all Jews had been ejected from England in 1290, as they were from France a century later in 1394. Spain expelled all its Jews in 1492, except for those who were baptized, and Portugal followed suit in 1497. Germany, being politically divided into scores of independent governments, kicked out Jews erratically and locally. As often as they were expelled, they would be invited back later to provide the one service they could provide in the middle ages: moneylending. Having just been kicked out of somewhere else, they would usually return. Jews became the wandering people of Augustine's rhetoric.

Jews in Christian Law

The images of Jews in Christian rhetoric were enacted in church law. Councils of the church passed canons (rules) to regulate Christian behavior and offer guidance on various problems that arose in the life of the church.

The first council to pass laws concerning relations between Jews and Christians met in Elvira, Spain, about the year 306. Of the eighty-one canons it passed, four dealt with Jews. Canon 16 decreed that "Catholic girls may not marry Jews or heretics." Canon 49 forbade landlords from allowing Jews "to bless the crops they have received from God." Canon 50 pronounced: "If any cleric or layperson eats with Jews, he or she shall be kept from communion as a way of correction," a decree repeated by the Council of Chalcedon in 451. Canon 78 decreed that any Christian male confessing adultery with a Jewish woman must be "denied communion for some time" (Elvira: 76, 79, 82). The bishops of Elvira sought to put an end to ordinary relationships between Christians and Jews.

Through the fifteenth century, councils of the church passed laws defining relations between Christians and Jews and limiting participation by Jews in the social and economic life of the people. The result was to incorporate the negative image of Jews into the fabric of the society and economy. The Council of Antioch (341) banned Christians from eating Passover with Jews. The Council of Laodicea (360) instructed Christians to work on the Sabbath, not to accept gifts of unleavened bread from Jews, and to avoid Jewish feasts. The Apostolic Canons (latter fourth century) prohibited Christians from entering synagogues. The Council of Agde (506) required Christians to fast on the Sabbath in Lent, to make the Sabbath less appealing to them. The Third Council of Orleans (538) proscribed Jews from mixing with Christians during Holy Week. In 581 the Council of Macon banned Jews from talking with nuns, from being judges, and from converting slaves to Judaism. The Council at Narbonne (589) barred Jews from working on Sunday and from singing the Psalms at funerals.

In the seventh century, the Council of Paris (614) declared that Jews seeking positions of authority must be baptized. The Council of Toledo IV (633) required Jewish children to be brought up by Christians, banned communication between baptized and unbaptized Jews, excluded Jews and Jewish Christians from holding public office, and prohibited Jews from owning Christian slaves (Christians were not so banned). The Council of Toledo VI (638) required Jews remaining in Spain to be baptized. The Council of Toledo IX (655) mandated church officials to oversee Jews during Jewish and Christian festivals. The XVIIth Council of Toledo (694) decreed that Jews in all regions of Spain but one must be reduced to slavery.

Christians were forbidden from visiting Jewish doctors or living in Jewish homes (Council of Narbonne, 1050) and Jews were required to pay tithes to support the church (Council of Gerona, 1078). Jews could not be plaintiffs or witnesses against Christians in court cases (Third Lateran Council, 1178), build new synagogues (Council of Oxford, 1222), nor obtain academic degrees (Council of Basel, 1434). Ghettos were declared compulsory for Jews in 1267 (Synod of Breslau). Jews were required to "be marked off . . . from other peoples through the character of their dress" by the Fourth Lateran Council held in Rome in 1215 (Parkes: 379-391). The purpose of this law was to make Jews more easily ostracized.

The effect of the anti-Jewish laws was to exclude Jews from participating in ordinary social, economic, and political life. Socially, they were outcasts. Economically, they were shut out from agriculture and from industry, both of which required some use of slave labor. Christians were allowed to own slaves; Jews were not. Politically, their rights were narrowed and eliminated to the point where they had none in a Christian society. Religiously, the ban against building and repairing synagogues was aimed at either destroying Judaism or making it live up to its image in the anti-Jewish literature.

Jews in the Christian State

The images of Jews articulated in Christian rhetoric and enacted in church law were quickly incorporated into the fabric of Christian society through actions of the state. Under the first significant Christian emperor, Theodosius II (408-450 C.E.), all the prevailing anti-Jewish church laws were included in his code of laws, which in turn became the basis of state law in Europe throughout the Middle Ages (Roth: 144). The popes, beginning with Gregory the Great (590-604 C.E.), sought to enforce a policy that prohibited persecuting Jews and forcibly baptizing them but which otherwise observed all the limitations placed on Jews by the laws of church and state.

The farther away a kingdom was from Rome, the less effective was papal restraint on active persecution of Jews. The eastern emperor Heraclius (610-641 C.E.) completely vetoed the public practice of Judaism. In France, local bishops led a series of attacks on Jews leading on occasion to forced baptisms. In the early seventh century the king of France ordered all Jews to be forcibly expelled from the country unless they converted. The king of Spain banned Jews from the economy, from seeking converts, from intermarrying with Christians, and from any position of authority or trust in the state. The law allowing Jewish children to be kidnapped and brought up by Christians was enforced (Roth: 147).

The Shadow of the Cross

Toward the end of the eleventh century, European Christians were outraged by reports coming from Christian pilgrims to the Holy Land. Palestine was under Muslim control. Pilgrims told stories of murder, robbery, and offenses committed against the holy places of Christian devotion. Anger grew until Pope Urban II in 1095 preached a crusade to retake the Holy Land from "the infidel" (Pawlikowski: 144). The first crusade was launched the next year, and the knights who led it regarded themselves as "God's avengers." At place after place along the Rhine valley, Jewish communities were attacked and exterminated; some Jews who submitted to baptism were spared. When the first crusaders reached Jerusalem, they herded all the Jews there into one of the synagogues and set it on fire. This pattern continued as long as the crusades lasted. During the third crusade, anti-Jewish contagion infected England with the ravage of London Jewry and the murder of Jews in many English cities (Roth: 183).

The aftermath of the crusades witnessed a rise in anti-Jewish feeling in Europe. New and even more negative images of Jews were spread abroad, perhaps out of a deep if perverted awareness that something awful was required to justify the mass murder of Jews on the crusades. Jews were now accused of *ritual murder*, of *desecrating the host*, and of *well poisoning*.

Ritual murder was the slander that Jews kill a Christian child every spring to obtain blood for use in the Passover. This libel was repeated throughout the middle ages and into the twentieth century; untold thousands of Jews have died because of it. Needless to say, it is a total fabrication.

Host desecration claims that Jews steal communion wafers in which Christ was believed to be bodily present and stab them with knives, seeking to crucify him again. The wafer would bleed, a miracle would occur, the Jew would be converted, and a public outcry would arise. Then the Jewish community would be attacked. Again, much death would result.

The charge of well poisoning was introduced to "explain" the outbreak of the Black Death in the fourteenth century. Jews were said to have caused it by concocting a poison made from communion wafers, human hearts and blood, frogs, spiders, lizards, and urine, which they threw into the wells of Christians. Massacres and mass lynchings followed; six thousand Jews were killed at Mainz when the Jewish quarter of the city was set afire.

Jews, Satan, and Women

Today, visitors to Rome can visit the Church of St. Peter in Chains, where they can see Michelangelo's sculptures for the tomb of Pope Julius II. The centerpiece is a sculpture of Moses with two horns on his head. The earliest link between Jews and the devil was made in John 8:44; in the later middle ages it was popularly believed that Jews had horns and a tail. As the slanders that Jews murdered Christian children, violated communion wafers, and poisoned wells show, the idea that they do the devil's work was now commonly held. The old notion that Jews are more carnal, less spiritual than Christians, and that the synagogue is a brothel, formed a three-way link between Jews, women, and the devil.

The Hammer Against Witches, published in 1486, was a handbook to guide inquisitors in seeking out witches. In it women

64

were accused of being lightminded, fickle, feeble in intelligence, quick to waver in faith, and cursed with an insatiable sexual desire to the extent that they lusted for intercourse with the devil (Kraemer: 122). Together with Jews and the devil, women kept "the witches' sabbath." Like Jews, they symbolized impurity, carnality, weakness, and temptation; tens of thousands of women were executed in the campaign against witchcraft. Like women, Jews were thought of as less than fully human, to be scorned, loathed, and mocked. Women and Jews practiced sorcery and magic, so it was said.

Jews As Usurers

As a result of church and state law, Jews were forced out of all ways of participating in the economy except two: dealing in old clothes and lending money. Church law forbade Christians to lend money at interest, but as society became dependent on money, the need arose to have someone perform this function. Just when the Jews were excluded from ordinary means of making a living, they found an opportunity in the most unpopular way of doing so: moneylending (Roth: 193). For some time Jews were the only capitalists in medieval countries. Money had to be obtained for building projects and for raising armies; indeed, Jews financed many crusaders. As Christians later moved into moneylending, Jews were confined to minor transactions, becoming little more than pawnbrokers.

Contemporary Images of Jews

The more extreme, vulgar medieval images of Jews have little currency among American Christians today. Yet a few years ago, a pastor made nationwide headlines by declaring that "God does not hear the prayers of a Jew." A recent sociological study of Christian attitudes discloses that negative images of Jews remain strongly present in the Christian mind. While 73 percent of American Protestants think of Jesus' apostles as Christians, 44 percent regard Judas, his betrayer, as a Jew. Seventy-nine percent think that Pilate wanted to avoid crucifying Jesus, while 58 percent hold the Jews most responsible for crucifying him (Glock: 47-54). Thirty-three percent of Protestants think that the Jews never can be forgiven for what they did to Jesus until they accept him as the savior, while 13 percent continue to affirm that the reason Jews have troubles is that God is punishing them for having rejected Jesus (Glock: 62-64). Twenty-five percent of Protestants think that being Jewish prevents people from being saved, while 38 percent still approve efforts to convert Jews (Glock: 78).

Non-religious negative images of Jews abound. Fifty-eight percent of Catholics think that Jews are wealthier than Christians; 48 percent of Protestants imagine that Jews dominate international banking. Opinion runs high that Jews control the television and movie industries, that they are less trustworthy in business than Christians, and that they have lower moral standards (Glock: 111). Forty percent of Protestants feel that Jews think of themselves as better than other people, and 68 percent of Catholics regard Jews as clannish. Significantly, 37 percent of Catholics and 44 percent of Protestants report that they have "unfriendly" feelings toward Jews with regard to the images named above. About 38 percent of Protestants and 31 percent of Catholics admit that they do not know a single Jew well (Glock: 157).

Hitler and the "Final Solution"

The Nazis set out to end the "Jewish problem" once and for all. They intended to provide a "final solution" (*Endlosung*) to the "Jewish question" by seeing to it that not one Jew was left on planet earth. The world was to be cleansed of Jews. That is why we refer to the destruction of roughly six million Jews as the "final solution." No other term captures the uniqueness of Nazi intentionality. We will not use the term "holocaust," because it means a "whole burnt offering" and refers to the means of grace in the sacrificial system.

Did It Really Happen?

On any topic, there is a lunatic fringe that announces that up is down and that left and right are indistinguishable from one another. With regard to the final solution, the lunatic fringe declares that the whirlwind of destruction unleashed upon European Jews by the Nazis never happened. Sometimes its representatives rewrite history to "prove" that the whole thing is nothing more than a "Jewish" fabrication.

Frequently, when I take part in a workshop on Jewish-Christian relations at a church assembly, a man walks to the front of the room after the discussion and shows me the snapshots he took of a concentration camp in the last days of World War II. Recently in Indiana a reunion was held between concentration camp survivors and military veterans who were rescuers. The veterans brought their pictures. The Nazis were embarrassingly good record keepers and picture takers. At the National Archives in Washington, D.C., there are millions of documents testifying to the final solution. Editions of the documents are available (Dawidowicz), as are examples of the pictures (Cargas). It happened.

Why So Little Christian Resistance?

The record of Christian behavior under the Nazis is decidedly mixed. Christians of every denomination either knuckled under to Hitler or cooperated with him. Three major movements known as the "German Christians" strongly supported Hitler. Yet, opposition can be found among Protestants and Roman Catholics. The most well known group of Protestant resisters was the "Confessing Church," with which Karl Barth and Dietrich Bonhoeffer were associated. Those who cooperated with Hitler vastly outnumbered the resisters, and even those who resisted often failed to see the issues clearly.

When we ask why there was not more resistance, we receive several answers. Resistance required heroism, and most people are not heroic. Knowing that helping a Jewish family will endanger one's own family would be quite enough to stop most of us from being heroic. That's the first answer—heroism is rare. If we are to prevent outbreaks of anti-Jewish action, we have to teach respect for Jews and Judaism ahead of time. If we wait until heroic action is our only option, we will once again have waited too long. We are now without excuse for knowing that the teaching of contempt has murderous consequences. We also know that we live in a world where mass murder on a grand scale is possible. The time to begin the teaching of respect is now.

The second answer is that the tradition of the teaching and practice of contempt itself contributed to either an active cooperation with Hitler or a lack of resistance to the final solution. In the parts of Europe that the Nazis controlled, the degree to which they successfully victimized Jews was directly correlated with the extent of anti-Judaism prevalent there before the war (Rubenstein: 217). Where traditional Christian anti-Judaism was intense, as in Poland, the policies of mass extermination were more successful. Where it was far less intense, as in Denmark, the policies either failed or were less successful. This is the second answer—the church's teaching of contempt made resistance difficult if not impossible.

The third answer has to do with Germany's churches. They had vigorously supported the nation in the First World War, which Germany had lost. That loss was followed by severe economic distress (deep depression and uncontrollable inflation), heavy financial obligations to the victors, and a government—the Weimar Republic—which had been more imposed on than sought by the people. The churches had a problem: The people did not find them trustworthy. Their nationalism was suspect. Protestants charged Catholics with being more loyal to the Pope than to "the fatherland." Mainstream German churches of all kinds decided to preach a new form of an old message: nationalism. Christian leaders urged devotion to the welfare of the German people: *das Volk.* "One additional target helped the churches to recoup: The Jews" (Rubenstein: 202). Again the mainline churches played their ancient role, seeking to regain their credibility at the expense of Jews.

The fourth answer also has to do with the church's teaching and practice of contempt, which had stripped away any sense that Jews are within the universe of moral obligation of Christians. The parable of the Good Samaritan tells us that the Samaritan let need—not race, class, or creed—define his universe of obligation. The result of two millennia of contempt, however, left Jews outside the universe of moral obligation for many Christians. Again, the teaching of contempt is a reason why there was little resistance to Hitler.

Forerunners of a New Era

If there was little resistance to Hitler, however, there was some. We may look upon those who did resist, even ambiguously,

68

as harbingers of a new day in relations between Christians and Jews.

Paul Tillich resisted Hitler. In 1932, a year before the Nazis came to power, Tillich wrote and published *The Socialist Decision*, in which he sought to prevent the triumph of Nazism by creating a political alternative to it. His friends recall that his public moral statements stamped him as a foe of the Nazis. The statement that led to his being the first Protestant fired by Hitler was a 1933 lecture on the contributions of major Jewish thinkers to German thought. Afterwards, Tillich heard one of his colleagues say, "Now they even want to turn us into Jews" (Friedlander: 176). Shortly, Tillich was ousted from his teaching position.

Dietrich Bonhoeffer is the most well-known Protestant resister. In 1944 he participated in a plot to assassinate Hitler; it failed and Bonhoeffer was hanged days before Germany surrendered in 1945. Bonhoeffer was a leader of the Confessing Church, which at its height included about one-third of the Protestant clergy in Germany. In May, 1934, this church issued the Barmen Declaration, denouncing the heresy of the "German Christians," their embracing of Nazi anti-Semitism (Barmen: 519). Yet, Barmen did not directly address the Jewish question.

Also prior to the Nazis' rise to power, Karl Barth protested against their policies. In 1928, he and Tillich signed a statement declaring the anti-Semitic movement incompatible with the Christian faith. In 1933, Barth preached a courageous sermon arguing that one cannot believe in Jesus Christ, himself a Jew, and be involved in the contempt for and ill treatment of Jews "which is now the order of the day" (Rubenstein: 205). In 1934, Barth was dismissed from his teaching post. Later he regretted not having made the Jewish issue central to the Barmen Declaration (Bethge: 167).

Among Roman Catholics, Cardinal Faulhaber protested against persecution of the church and against an Aryanized Christianity, although his protest was limited. Father Bernhard Lichtenberg prayed publicly for Jews in the Cathedral in Berlin; he died on the way to Dachau. Alfred Delp was hanged for resisting Hitler. Thousands of Catholic clergy were imprisoned for resisting Hitler. In Turkey, Angelo Roncalli, later to become Pope John XXIII, participated in "Operation Baptism" to provide phony baptismal certificates to Hungarian Jews. The Eastern Orthodox Church in Bulgaria and the Lutheran Church in Denmark were the brightest spots in Europe in helping Jews to survive. Resistance in both places was successful, but both situations were different for other reasons as well.

How should we regard the protesters? There are several wrong answers to the question. One is to condemn them for the inadequacy of their protest. All of those who survived long ago confessed that they should have done more. Another is to appeal to them as a justification for not taking Christian anti-Judaism seriously. This is a widespread (if more implicit than explicit) misuse of the witness of Roncalli and Tillich, as if to say that because of them we know that there is "really" no problem of Christian anti-Judaism. So to misuse the witness of a Lichtenberg and a Bonhoeffer is to be blind to the reasons for the mass darkness that was able to overcome all but a few flickering lights.

Instead we should see them as reminders to us of the gospel of Jesus Christ, of the promise of the love of God offered freely to each and all (therefore including the Jews) and of the command of God that justice be done to each and all of those whom God loves (therefore including the Jews). This gospel comes to us now as a challenge, setting before us the decision whether we will engage in the teaching and practice of respect, which God both gives and demands.

5

When Jews and Christians Meet

Dialogue with Jews

In order to learn respect for their Jewish neighbors, Christians should get to know them. As was pointed out earlier, the number of Christians who actually know at least one Jew well is quite small. Some congregations have taken steps to reverse this situation and have established regular avenues of conversation and celebration with neighboring Jewish congregations. Visits to each other's services of worship, pulpit exchanges, mutual participation in the high points of the liturgical year, and the establishment of dialogue groups will go a long way to take us beyond the teaching of contempt.

Perhaps this movement might lead us to learn respect for our neighbors and beyond even that, to a kind of interchange that would permit the faith of each party to be deepened by an enhanced awareness of the faith of the other. If so, we would move beyond dialogue to a process of "crossing over and coming back" (Cobb: 75). Were we to appreciate the Jewish witness of faith well enough to understand it empathetically, we would find that certain biblical dimensions of faith which we have downplayed would be reinvigorated within the Christian life itself. Had we faith enough to "let go," we would find our faith handed back to us, deepened.

Knowing the Other

The aim of this chapter is to describe the contemporary meeting between Jews and Christians in order to facilitate this kind of interchange. As a minority group in a predominantly Christian culture, less than forty-five years after the "final solution," Jews are concerned with matters not immediately important to Christians. For that matter, Christians have on their agendas issues less than momentous to Jews. Being clear about these differences is helpful.

Also, other issues complicate matters. One is the state of Israel, which we will take up in the next chapter. Another is women's issues, that feminist criticism that calls both traditional Judaism and traditional Christianity into question and therefore demands attention here. Additionally, there are four major sectors or "denominations" within Judaism, about which Christians need to be informed. Further, the very nature of Jewishness is such that one need not "believe" to be a Jew, which contrasts with Christianity, in which one participates (at least in theory) by believing. We shall try to throw some light on these dimensions of the contemporary meeting between Jews and Christians.

Jews Are a "People"

Were we to hazard a definition of Christianity or say what it means to be a Christian, we would find ourselves immediately thrown into a discussion of belief. At the heart of Christian self-definition is a creed, and this is true even of those churches that claim to have no such thing. At some point or other in the Christian life, whether before baptism in churches that baptize believers or at confirmation in churches that baptize infants, one must stand before the congregation and confess the Christian faith, professing belief in Jesus Christ. The word "creed" comes from the Latin *credo*, "I believe." Believing is inherent in being a Christian.

With Judaism, things are different. Theology, Jews like to say, is more important to Christians than to Jews (although here, a Christian theologian might say, Jews may overestimate the importance of theology to Christians). Yet, one way to formulate the difference between Jews and Christians is to point out that Christianity is a "religion," whereas for Jews the term "religion" only partially fits the reality of Judaism. Even the term "Judaism," taken as referring to the religion of Jews, is a comparative new-

72

comer to Jewish vocabulary (Lange: 4). The Hebrew language has no word identical with the typical Christian meaning of "Judaism." Rather, being a Jew means "first and foremost to belong to a group, the Jewish people, and the religious beliefs are secondary, in a sense, to this corporate allegiance" (Lange: 4). Jewishness is fundamentally a matter of loyalty to the Jewish people, a loyalty professed by many who claim to have no religious beliefs at all.

One way of making this point is to note that a Jew is a Jew by virtue of being born into the Jewish people, whereas "it is by virtue of a decision or confession that a Christian *becomes* a Christian" (Eckardt: 4). Jewish identity is *laic* (from the Greek word *laos*, people), by which we are not to understand merely "ethnic" or "racial," but a people comprising "a great variety of ethnic backgrounds and racial differences" (Eckardt: 5).

It is most important for Christians to understand that Jews are not in any sense of the word a "race." The *Falasha* Jews, for example, are Ethiopian blacks who claim roots going back to the biblical era. On the other hand, *Ashkenazic* Jews are of central and eastern European origin. While conversions to Judaism are discouraged (a situation that is undergoing some change), they do take place, and a member of any ethnic group may become a Jew. Sammy Davis, Jr. and Elizabeth Taylor are Jews by conversion, members of the Jewish people but not Jews by race.

The insistence that Jews are a race was the centerpiece of Nazi policy, and the Nazis labored intensely at defining "scientifically" just what "racial" characteristics constituted Jewishness. Notably, they failed (Hilberg: 39-54). The vain attempt of the Nazis to define Jews as a race leads us to an important qualification of the remark that Jews cannot be defined religiously or by belief. The Nazis finally defined a "Jew" by reference to the religious practice, belief, or faithfulness of one's grandparents. A person with one grandparent who had remained a faithful Jew was defined as a Jew.

Hence, while belief is not essential to being Jewish, neither is it escapable. Jewish identity involves, first, peoplehood, and within that peoplehood a faith. The faith is not unimportant. A Jewish atheist likely had faithful Jewish grandparents or parents and will likely not have Jewish grandchildren. Consequently, one thing that Christians can say to Jews these days is that they should not neglect the task of theological reflection, of appropriating their tradition in a healthy and critical way. A great danger of Jews in America today is that young people will drift away from Judaism for lack of a convincing intellectual articulation of the meaning of Jewish faith.

It is equally important to point out that, as Jews are not a "race," neither has being a Jew anything to do with racism. "Judaism is virtually oblivious to race" (Greenstein: 97). Converts to Judaism from every ethnic or racial group enjoy equal status with every Jew who was born into the covenant. Jews are a people comprised of many peoples, not unlike Americans.

Guilt and Suspicion

When Jews and Christians meet, they do so as equal human beings who have the right to expect from each other the respect for one another's dignity that should characterize all civil relations among people. In another sense, however, we do not meet as equals. To any encounter between Jews and Christians, Jews tend to bring at least a trace of apprehension or mistrust that is difficult to overcome. On the whole, Jews are far more aware of the history of Christian treatment of Jews than Christians are.

By the same token, Christians who come to the encounter with Jews are likely to be people who have become aware of this history and who, therefore, cannot avoid being embarrassed by it. "The Christian side carries moral scars and moral afflictions that are not found on the Jewish side" (Eckardt: 8). Consequently, Jews and Christians bring different expectations to the meeting between Christians and Jews. Along with a vision of a better future between Jews and Christians, Jews will be concerned with securing and maintaining their own interests and integrity as a religious and ethnic minority. Christians, on the other hand, are likely to wonder what they can do to make amends for and subdue the history of tribulation that Christians have visited upon Jews.

If there is to be a better future for Jews and Christians in their relation with one another, Jews will have to learn how to deal with their suspicion and Christians with their guilt (or guilt feelings). Jews would probably be unwise to let go entirely of their suspicion, since few Christians have faced up to their anti-Judaism and overcome it. They could, however, benefit from distinguishing between healthy and unhealthy suspicion. The latter tends toward delusions of persecution and finds evidence to confirm its view where such evidence does not exist. Healthy suspicion would accept Christians at face value while being mindful that anti-Judaism remains a threat.

How should Christians deal with guilt—or, more properly, guilt feelings—for the Christian past? A variety of answers to this question come to mind. Marvin Wilson, an evangelical Christian theologian, argues that Christians should recognize the legitimacy of their guilt and repent of it. The problem of Christian anti-Judaism cannot be solved by education alone. Declares Wilson: "For two thousand years the church has stuck its bony finger in the Jew's face and said, 'You repent!' but I am not sure the church has faced up to the need for its own repentance" (Stallsworth: 93). Other Christians are less sure that Christians need to repent. Richard John Neuhaus, a Lutheran theologian, finds "an artificiality in Jewish-Christian relations at this point" (Stallsworth: 93). He does not think it will strengthen relations between Christians and Jews if Christians "jump through the hoops of self-degradation," if all the obligations in dialogue between Jews and Christians fall on the shoulders of Christians.

Wilson and Neuhaus each make good points. Christians must transcend their inherited anti-Judaism, and that cannot be done without confronting it. No Christian seriously participates in the effort to transform Christianity or engage in constructive relations with Jews without repenting of the past. Jumping through hoops of self-degradation is a different matter, something we can do without genuinely repenting. In fact, it can lead to the opposite, a reinstatement of nasty attitudes toward Jews. We do not much like those before whom we are required to engage in self-abasement. Nor can healthy relationships be based on the humiliation of one partner.

Here Jewish wisdom can be helpful. Rabbi Milton Himmelfarb advocates moderation in all things, guilt included. With Rabbinic humor he suggests that if "there are Christians who wallow in guilt, then they are enjoying their guilt too much" (Stallsworth: 94). Being what he calls "a good ascetic," Himmelfarb does not think that people should enjoy themselves too much. He helps us see that a preoccupation with guilt can simply be a way of thinking more about ourselves than about our neighbors.

Rabbi David Novak points out that the three major kinds of Christianity—Catholic, Protestant, and Orthodox—have in each case radically diverse histories of resisting the persecution of Jews in the Nazi era. Catholics in Italy, Protestants in Denmark, and Orthodox in Bulgaria made highly impressive records of saving Jews. By the same token, the records of Catholics in Poland, Protestants in Germany, and Orthodox in the Ukraine were abominable (Stallsworth: 95). Some Christians persecuted Jews, some resisted such persecution. Novak compares charges against Christians today of complicity in the final solution with Christian charges against Jews for the execution of Jesus. The fact that *some* Jews were involved in Jesus' unjust murder means that only those so involved were guilty. Certainly, Jews of a later time are not guilty of it. The same argument applies to charges of Christian guilt in the final solution. Such charges are as "morally illegitimate" as are the charges of deicide against Jews (Stallsworth: 96).

Rabbi Ronald B. Sobel contends that the idea that Christians today are responsible for what Christians of an earlier time did to Jews in Spain in 1492, in Poland in 1648, or in Germany in 1939 is as "morally reprehensible as the idea that all Jews are responsible for . . . the death of Jesus" (Stallsworth: 97). What Jews want from Christians today is not guilt and certainly not groveling; rather, they would like Christians to undo what Christendom has done. What Christendom did was the teaching and practice of contempt; to undo it we must teach and practice respect.

Jews Are a Minority Group

American Christians have great difficulty imagining what it must be like to live in a country in which they are a religious minority and in which the religion of the majority is socially and culturally, if not politically, established. Even the frequent appeals that Christians make to the "early church" fail to note that part of its dilemma was that it existed in such a situation. To understand Jews calls for us to transcend this limitation, because Jews are as conscious of being a religious minority in America as American Christians would be if transported to India.

Given their minority status, Jews have pronounced views on

relations between church and state, although their views are by no means uniform. On the one hand, Jews overall "are probably more devoted than anyone else in America to the separation of church and state" (Himmelfarb: 1). A 1984 survey of Jewish opinions found that two out of every three Jews oppose tuition tax credits for parents of children in private and parochial schools or for parents of children in Jewish day schools. Three out of four opposed "a moment of silent meditation each day in the public schools" (Himmelfarb: 1). To most Jews, school prayers mean "prayers of other people's faiths . . . and reemphasis of our status as a 'minority' religion" (Himmelfarb: 6).

Three out of four Jews oppose "teaching *about* [not *of*] religion in the public schools" (Himmelfarb: 2). Also, Jewish voting patterns are "liberal" by American standards. Most of them vote markedly to the left of their bankbooks, i.e., they "live like Episcopalians and vote like Puerto Ricans" (Eckardt: 48). This, however, is not the whole story.

Protestants would do well to remember that in American church history for more than three centuries we drew inspiration from the vision of a Christian America. Benjamin Franklin thought that there should be nondenominational prayers at the Constitutional Convention in 1787, and President Eisenhower affirmed that our form of government "is founded in a deeply felt religious faith, and I don't care what it is" (Sarna: 11). Consequently, throughout most of American history Jews have not sought separation of church and state but equal treatment of different religions by the state—a state that would be neutral to all religions rather than divorced from all religions.

It was only as the plea for equal treatment increasingly fell on deaf ears that Jews, in the late nineteenth century, began to seek safety in the doctrine of strict separation (Sarna: 15). Then they began to appeal not to Benjamin Franklin but to Thomas Jefferson, who interpreted the first amendment as a "wall of separation between church and state" and refused to proclaim Thanksgiving Day lest he "indirectly assume to the United States an authority over religious exercises" (Sarna: 15).

It is probably fair to say that today the separationist consensus among American Jews has, in its turn, broken down. Jews and Christians face a similar dilemma. History teaches Jews two contradictory lessons: that separation of church and state is their best defense against a state dominated by Christians and, on the contrary, that secularism is a force leading to assimilation, moral decay, and persecution of religions, Judaism included (Sarna: 19).

One can see this dilemma played out at Christmas, a time that presents particular difficulties to Jews. Christmas is both a Christian holiday and a national holiday, but it is not an American holiday in the same sense as the Fourth of July. Yet we have a national Christmas tree at the White House and a national proclamation, plus Christmas decorations in many public places.

How should we respond to this situation? Those who follow a strict separationist, Jeffersonian agenda, are apt to file suit to remove all religious symbols from state-owned property. Those who think that government should treat all religions equally seek to place a *menorah* (the nine-branched candelabrum used at Hanukkah) alongside the Christmas tree.

Christians concerned for better relations with Jews need to take the questions involved in church-state issues with a greater seriousness. The worst chapters of Christian history involved the establishment of the church (which always meant some particular church) by the state, which brought with it persecution not only of Jews but of all kinds of Christians other than the establishment variety. The church was too long learning that it cannot be both ultimately dependent on God and dependent on the state, although reformers like Thomas and Alexander Campbell typified many Americans in advocating a thoroughgoing reclamation of liberty "in all things civil and religious" (Osborn: 24). Christians in America today are apt to be lethargic in their enjoyment of a liberty for which their forebears struggled. Perhaps one benefit of better understanding of Jews would be to recall to us an awareness of the importance of religious liberty to which so many of our traditions witness.

Women: Jewish and Christian

Of the factors that complicate relations between Christians and Jews today, perhaps none is more significant than the rise of the women's movement, which calls both Christianity and Judaism into question for the sexism that is present in each tradition. That things are changing with regard to how women are treated in Judaism today is reflected in the fact that three of its four branches (Reform, Conservative, and Reconstructionist) ordain women to the rabbinate. Reform Judaism has ordained women since 1972, and Conservative Judaism since 1985; Reconstructionism freely ordains women (Raphael: 69).

Meanwhile, in Christianity, most "mainline" Protestant churches ordain women, although some do not and some do in some countries but not others (e.g., the Anglican tradition). The Roman Catholic and Eastern Orthodox churches do not ordain women. The Southern Baptist Convention opposes women's ordination, but there are, nevertheless, several hundred Southern Baptist clergywomen. Here we shall look first at the strengths of the Jewish tradition with regard to women, next at the weaknesses, and then at a problem that Jewish feminists have with some Christian feminists.

Long ago, Reform Judaism originated the service of confirmation for young people (men and women) as a replacement for the traditional *bar mitzvah* ("son of the commandment") ceremony that marks a *young man's* coming of age (Greenstein: 56). The principle involved was that of equal rights for women and men. This practice has now spilled over to other branches of Judaism as well, so that now both *bar* and *bat mitzvah* ("daughter of the commandment") services are held, with confirmation taking place at a slightly later age as a statement of a continuing search for fulfillment in Judaism.

Similarly, many Reform congregations have also introduced an expanded service on the occasion of the birth of a girl, to parallel the ceremonies in the synagogue and home surrounding the circumcision of a boy, his entrance into the "covenant of circumcision." The service for girls is a *b'rit chayim* (a "covenant of life" ritual), and both female and male children are presented in the synagogue on Shabbat shortly after birth (Greenstein: 74).

All traditional religions were structured on the pattern of patriarchy ("rule by the fathers"), Judaism no less so than Christianity. Yet Judaism for most of its history, patriarchal as it was, has the better record on the treatment of women. Marriage could take place only by mutual consent, could be consummated only by mutual consent, and sexuality was regarded as healthful and necessary. It was not shameful, and marriage was not an option "second-best" to celibacy. Nor was the only legitimate purpose of sex that of producing children, as the Christian tradition long maintained.

Contraceptive methods were permitted or required if the woman's life or child's health were at risk, and both wives and husbands had the right of divorce for a variety of rather liberal reasons (Greenstein: 77-80). Technically, men could divorce women but not vice-versa, but the rabbinic courts could get around this by granting a wife's petition to do so. On the whole, however, divorce was, at least until recently, fairly rare among Jews, partly because marriage among Jews tended to be rather wholesome. The right of divorce and a marriage contract have been available in Judaism since Talmudic times, and only recently in a Christian context.

Whereas all this compares rather favorably to much of the Christian tradition, which bought into Aristotle's definition of woman as a "misbegotten male" (Thomas Aquinas: 95), that does not mean that Judaism is without serious weaknesses in its traditional stance toward women. The source of these weaknesses is that women were required to observe only the negative commandments of Judaism; they were "excused" from the positive ones. Being "excused" meant that women were free to stay at home and not "required" to participate in the life of the synagogue. Rachel Adler, a Jewish feminist, created the term "peripheral Jews" to describe the category in which women were placed along with children and Canaanite slaves.

Commenting on this situation, Adler remarks that slaves could be freed and become full Jews and that children could grow up and become full Jews, "only women can never grow up, or be freed or otherwise leave the category" (cited in Eckardt: 122). Adler, however, does not grant Christianity any greater moral credibility on the subject of women. The Hebrew Bible, she notes, regards only males as full-fledged members of the Jewish people and refers to Israel as a "harlot" when *she* sins. Whereas the New Testament hints at the equality of the sexes, it ends, in the Book of Revelation, "by presenting a vision of white-garbed men enjoying proximity to the throne of God because they have not 'defiled' themselves with women" (cited in Eckardt: 123).

Adler illustrates the fact that Jewish feminists criticize Judaism for its traditional patriarchy and sexism. They do this, however, without engaging in anti-Judaism, which brings us to the topic of the teaching of contempt for Judaism by Christian feminists. The contention made here is that some women are Jews and about half of all Jews are women. Therefore, a Christian feminist position cannot be both pro-women and anti-Jewish. Yet this is exactly what Jewish feminists detect in a number of Christian feminists.

Judith Plaskow delineates "a new myth" circulating among Christian feminists, a myth that credits the ancient Hebrews with inventing patriarchy after an earlier matriarchal period. The "new myth" goes on to say that Jesus attempted to re-establish egalitarianism, an effort that was thwarted by the endurance of Jewish attitudes within the Christian tradition. This myth, Plaskow states, "perpetuates traditional Christianity's negative picture of Judaism by attributing sexist attitudes to Christianity's Jewish origins" (Plaskow: 306). The result is that "feminism is turned into another weapon in the Christian anti-Judaic arsenal" (Plaskow: 306). Christianity is again defined, as the church fathers defined it, as other than Jewish and better than Jewish.

The unfortunate appearance of anti-Judaism in Christian feminists turns upon their interpretation of the figure of Jesus. Studies claiming to describe his attitudes toward women draw the bleakest possible picture of the situation of women in Judaism in order to make Jesus' attitudes stand out by contrast. As Plaskow sees it, these studies commit three serious scholarly blunders. First, they regularly regard attitudes found in the Talmud and rabbinic literature from a much later period (as late as 600 C.E.) as describing Jewish attitudes in the time of Jesus (Plaskow: 306). Second, they treat rabbinic views as monolithic and regularly select "only the most negative rabbinic passages on the topic," ignoring all the very positive ones (Plaskow: 307). Third, they compare the teachings of "an itinerant preacher" (Jesus) with "sayings formulated in the rarefied atmosphere of rabbinic academies" (Plaskow: 307), ignoring rabbinic statements that are clearly parallel to those of Jesus.

Plaskow's view of the place of women in the two faiths is that both associated women with sexuality and fear woman as temptress. They responded to this situation differently, with Christianity compensating for the image of the temptress with that of the virgin; the "perfect" woman would be celibate. Judaism compensated "with the good wife with whom sex is permitted and even encouraged" (Plaskow: 608). The two traditions offered women different opportunities and stuck them with different disabilities, but Plaskow thinks it would be "pointless to label one superior to the other" (Plaskow: 308).

Where her criticism of Christian feminists really hits home is in Plaskow's charge that such views indicate "a profound failure of the feminist ethic" (Plaskow: 308). By contrast to the morality of patriarchy, which failed to own that part of the psyche which it then projected onto the alien other, the feminist ethic is grounded on the "withdrawal of projection and the recognition that the full humanity of each of us embraces those despised characteristics patriarchy ascribed to a host of 'Others'" (Plaskow: 308). The persistence of anti-Judaism among Christian feminists, however, "represents precisely the continuation of a patriarchal ethic of projection" (Plaskow: 308). To be precise, Christian feminism projects onto Judaism Christianity's failure to overcome sexism. Plaskow calls to the attention of Christian feminists the fact that the fate of women and Jews rose and fell together in the history of Christendom: "When the Inquisition ran out of Jews, it persecuted witches—and vice versa" (Plaskow: 308).

Plaskow's criticism of Christian feminists shows that even well-intentioned thinkers will perpetuate an ideology, in this case the teaching of contempt, unless they take it explicitly into account. Unless redressed by Christian feminists, their failure to issue a corrective to anti-Judaism will poison any attempted meeting between Jews and Christians today. The most promising way around this difficulty is to focus on the good news of God's love offered freely to all—Jews included—and God's command that justice be done to all—Jews included, and quit trying to make of the historical Jesus the one whose life and teachings were against the Jews.

Branches of American Judaism

What kind of synagogue is that one down the street? Will our youth group be welcome there if we try to initiate an interfaith educational project with their congregation? Is the service all in Hebrew, mostly in English, or a mix of both? How much will I understand if I go there? Questions such as these are likely to occur to most American Christians considering entering into an interfaith dialogue or educational effort. In a few pages, we will look at the four major branches or sectors in American Judaism.

Reform Judaism started in Europe in the early nineteenth century, motivated by the goal of overcoming the gap that separated medieval Judaism from the developing modern world. Early reformers did not want to have to choose between being Jewish and medieval or modern but no longer Jewish. They were particularly concerned with what would happen to young people who came into contact with modern science and culture in the universities. Also they wanted to reconcile the requirements of the Jewish way (*Halakah* or "Law") with the new situation of Jews in the modern context. Antiquated commandments were to be dropped but not arbitrarily; *Halakah* was to be updated by the process of rabbinic discussion and decision-making.

Initially a few changes were made in worship and ritual. Sermons were to be preached in the local language, and organ music was introduced into the service along with musical accompaniment to singing. In America the reform process went further, with the dropping of Hebrew and the dietary laws, along with many traditional rituals. As part of the commitment to be both Jews and Americans, Zionist concerns to settle again in the land of Israel were also set aside. Weekly services were sometimes held on Sundays, and Sunday schools were introduced, as was the service of confirmation for both young women and men. The "mission" of Reform Judaism was largely redefined, in the light of the *Torah* and the prophets, as one of work for social justice for all people.

In these days, Reform Judaism continues to change. Since Hitler's "final solution," some decisions of early Reform Judaism have been questioned. More Hebrew is used in services now, although translations are provided in the prayer book. Affirmation of the state of Israel (Zionism) is quite important, and women are ordained as rabbis (Agus: 5-29).

The three pillars of Jewish life are God, *Torah*, and Israel (in the sense of the Jewish people). Each sector of Judaism lays primary emphasis on one pillar, though not to the neglect of the other two. Central to Reform Judaism are two ideas: that of God, understood as an ethical monotheism, and of Judaism as a developing faith. For *Conservative Judaism*, the stress is on

Israel, specifically on what one of its founders called "catholic Israel" (Greenstein: 122).

Conservative Judaism takes a moderate stance on matters of practice between Reform and Orthodoxy, seeking thereby to establish a broad base of unity among American Jews. Beginning in America, Conservative Judaism early introduced English prayers and sermons into the standard service but continued to emphasize the dietary laws, Zionism, the Sabbath observance, and the use of Hebrew. From the point of view of Conservative Judaism, Reform paid too little heed to *Torah* and Israel, limiting Judaism to reflection on God and ethics; and Orthodoxy was too fixated on the requirements of *Torah*, ignoring the needs of the Jewish people. Hence, Conservatives use English in worship, not out of a theological conviction but because of the recognition that most Jews simply do not know Hebrew well enough to understand a sermon preached in it. Conservatism combines Reform's emphasis on development with a deep respect for the Jewish past (Waxman: 247-257).

Having begun within Conservative Judaism, *Reconstructionism* has become a fourth movement in American Judaism. Most of its inspiration comes from the thought of one person, Mordecai M. Kaplan, who sought to carry out a radical "reconstruction" of belief and practice for contemporary Jews in order to stem the disintegration of Jewish life in America. Influenced by John Dewey, Kaplan regarded Judaism as a "civilization," the features of which are decided by the Jewish people. Whatever serves the historical continuity of Israel, whether dietary laws or the use of Hebrew, is to be prized not because it was immutably commanded by God but because of its social utility. Dietary customs are optional folkways that invest the act of eating with a spiritual quality.

Reconstructionism's most daring change has been to remove the idea of Israel as the "chosen people" and to replace it with the concept of Israel as an evolving religious civilization. Chosenness was rejected because it was taken to indicate that Jews thought themselves superior to other peoples. Like Reform, Reconstructionism places a high premium on the development of human beings to their full actualization and on social ethics (Greenstein: 136).

Whereas Reform emphasizes the idea of God as an ethical

84

monotheism, and Conservative and Reconstructionist Judaism stress the people Israel, Orthodoxy puts its emphasis on *Torah* or covenant, which it regards in its totality as the result of divine revelation. The *Torah* includes both the written and the oral *Torah* and the codification of these teachings in various rabbinic authorities respected by Orthodox Judaism. The requirements of Jewish law are rather strictly regarded, although some Orthodox rabbis will propose rather striking new forms of *Halakah*. Also, Orthodoxy is by no means monolithic, containing movements ranging from the Hasidim (praised by Martin Buber) to very liberal reinterpreters of Judaism.

For Orthodoxy, the traditional dietary laws (*kashrut* or *kosher*) are binding, whereas Reform Judaism has rejected the dietary rules as out of date. The qualification to be noted here is that while some Orthodox Jews will ignore some of the dietary laws, some Reform Jews will observe some of them. Conservatives will suggest testing each regulation to see whether it contributes to a significant religious life. Reconstructionists will be concerned with the role these laws have played in the life of the Jewish people, although they may disregard most of them. Theory and practice will vary widely within any branch of Judaism, as they do within Christian denominations.

Similarly, Orthodoxy will tend to be strict with regard to prohibiting anything on the Sabbath that is defined as work, while Reform drops the traditional regulations and leaves details up to the individual. Conservative Judaism will stress the positive Sabbath practices rather than the prohibitions, and Reconstructionism will urge consideration be given to what is fulfilling for individuals.

Diversity Rules

In sum, when Christians meet Jews they will encounter many different kinds of people, even within any given branch of Judaism. Attention to the rather wide variety of Christians within any one congregation or denomination should prepare us for the fact that neither Judaism nor any sector within it is monolithic. That will be part of what makes the meeting interesting.

6

Israel: Land and State

Facing Up to the Christian Tradition

Here we turn to deal with Israel today, as both a land and a state. We will not be concerned in this chapter with Israel so much as we will with *how we talk about* Israel. The purpose of this chapter is not to instruct readers as to what they should think about Israel but to articulate a perspective within which Israel can be discussed by Christians committed to overcoming the anti-Judaism of the Christian tradition.

Many Christians launch into a discussion of the state of Israel today with no consideration whether they have yet come to terms with the anti-Judaism in their own tradition. On the assumption that our thinking is shaped by traditions of which we are unaware, here we will look at the tradition of Christian anti-Judaism for what it has said about Israel as a land and a state, on which it has made rather definite remarks. Only when Christians have set our anti-Judaism resolutely to one side may we safely proceed to discuss Israel.

Spiritualizing Israel

The *adversus Judaeos* tradition has made two moves with regard to Israel. It has either spiritualized Israel, denying its status as a concrete land and place, or it has announced, in the name of God, that Jews have no right to live in the land of Israel. We see the spiritualizing tendency at least as early as the second century. The apostolic father, Barnabas, offered an interpretation of God's promise of the land of Israel. The first paragraph of Exodus 33 reads: "The Lord said to Moses, 'Depart, go up hence, you and the people whom you have brought up out of the land of Egypt, to the land of which I swore to Abraham, Isaac, and Jacob, saying, "To your descendants I will give it." . . . Go up to a land flowing with milk and honey.'" Wanting to deny the literal meaning of this passage, Barnabas began by asking himself the meaning of the words "a land flowing with milk and honey."

Barnabas' answer to his own question was ingenious. On his interpretation, "the good land" no longer refers to the land of Israel but to Jesus Christ. His reasoning, apparently, was that since the word "land" or "earth" in Hebrew is *adama*, and since "Adam" was so named because he was made from the earth, and since Christ is the "second Adam," it is he who is also the promised land. The promise, therefore, is no longer made to Jews, but to us: "We, then, are they whom He has led into the good land" (Barnabas: 141).

Turning his attention to the milk and honey that are supposed to flow freely in this good land, Barnabas asks after their meaning and declares that "as the infant is kept alive first by honey, and then by milk, so also we, being quickened and kept alive by the faith of the promise and by the word, shall live ruling over the earth" (Barnabas: 141). Here is Barnabas' exegesis: land = Christ; milk and honey = faith and the word. Barnabas' triumphalism is transparent in his claim that we shall rule the earth. As early as the second century, we see the truth of W.D. Davies' remark that "for the holiness of place, Christianity has fundamentally . . . substituted the holiness of Person: it has Christified holy space" (Davies: 368).

Proclaiming Jewish Homelessness

The second move made by the anti-Jewish ideology involved transcendentalizing the geo-politics of the ancient world. At the end of the second war with Rome in 135 C.E., the Emperor Hadrian issued a decree barring Jews from entering the city of Jerusalem. The city was renamed *Aelia Capitolina* (Capitol City) and dedicated to the god Jupiter, a statue of whom was placed on the spot where the Temple had stood (Finkelstein: 158). It was not long before Christian apologists seized upon the opportunities afforded them by this tragic turn of events.

Justin Martyr, writing in Rome around the middle of the second century, misused prophetic self-criticism of Israel to confer approval upon Hadrian's act. "Those who slandered Him [Christ]," declared Justin, "should be miserable" (Justin: 179). He explained that Jews suffer today not only because they are guilty of not having recognized the One with whom they had to do in their history, but also and chiefly because when he appeared among them, they killed him (Justin: 184). For this reason, Justin remarks to Jews, your land is "desolate, and your cities burned with fire, and . . . strangers may eat your fruit in your presence, and not one of you may go up to Jerusalem" (Justin: 202). This early is the deicide charge alleged as the reason for Jewish homelessness.

Irenaeus (ca. 130—ca. 200) was bishop of Lyons from about 178. His major work, *Against All Heresies*, attacks several major heresies of the time, including Marcionism, the movement which rejected the God of Israel, the creator God, as an inferior deity. Irenaeus was concerned to reject both Marcionism and Judaism, and thus had to perform a difficult tightrope act. He counteracted the Marcionite objection that Jerusalem would not have been destroyed had it not been the city of the God of Israel by contending that Jerusalem was "rightly forsaken" because the Jews (not God) "are no longer useful for bringing forth fruit" (Irenaeus: 466).

Tertullian (ca. 160—ca. 225), a North African church leader active in Carthage and second only to Augustine as the most infuential theologian in western Christianity prior to the Reformation, argued in his anti-Jewish tract that, because Jews have forsaken God in their rejection of Christ, it is "in accordance with their deserts" that they "should be prohibited from entering the holy city" (Tertullian: 174).

Origen, a biblical critic and theologian in the eastern church (ca. 185—ca. 254), repeated the theme of Jewish suffering and homelessness "on account of their unbelief and other insults which they heaped upon Jesus" (Origen: 433). He, too, transcendentalized the military turns of fortune of the ancient world declaring that "these calamities they have suffered because they were a most wicked nation, although guilty of many other sins,

88

yet has been punished so severely for none as for those that were committed against Jesus" (Origen: 433).

Earlier in this book we have looked at Augustine's well-known allegory on the story of Cain and Abel. Here we simply recall the conclusion of Augustine's interpretation: that like Cain, the Jews are condemned to witness to the fate of those who reject Christ by wandering across the face of the earth. They are to be preserved in a state of dispersal from home, that "to the end of the seven days of time" they will constitute "a proof to believing Christians of the subjection merited by those who . . . put the Lord to death" (Augustine: 32).

The Power of Tradition

Were it not for the influence on us of traditions of which we are hardly aware, all this would be little more than ancient history. Such, however, is far from the case. A conscientious Christian preacher today, turning to a standard biblical reference work to check on the meaning of the term "Israel," might well find the "Hebrew nation" of ancient Israel declared a failure for having fallen short of God's purposes for it. In this perspective, the prophets are interpreted as having looked forward "to the day in which God shall fashion a new instrument, more adequate to his purpose" (Richardson: 118). The author then claims that "all the NT writers regard the church . . . as this new instrument, and see the fulfillment of Israel's destiny in the new covenant." Hence, "the Christian Church is, in fact, the New Israel" (Richardson: 118). In this way, the views of Barnabas are passed along under the guise of New Testament scholarship, and no evidence is offered from the New Testament to back up the claim. Since the term "New Israel" never appears there, the interpretation is, at best, strained.

Christians holding such views, however vaguely they may be aware of them, will tend to think that the nation of Israel had its chance and failed, and has been replaced by the church. They may well wonder what right this nation has to be re-established today and why they should be concerned about its security and viability. Precisely such conclusions are drawn by Christians who make direct connections between the state of Israel today and traditional Christian anti-Judaism.

In his essay on "The Jewish Question and Zionism," Georg Fohrer claims that there is a clear relationship between the wrong way followed by second temple Judaism, that Judaism which recreated the Temple and the State of Israel after the Babylonian Exile, and all the later sufferings with which Jews were afflicted, even until today. This scholar contends that the re-establishment of Israel as a state, after the Exile and today, reflects nothing more than Israel's abandonment of its God-appointed task and the replacement of that task with a "typically human quest for enjoyment and security of life" (Fohrer, cited in Klein: 18). In the anti-Jewish tradition, attempts to create and secure the life of the State of Israel represent nothing more than the denial of what is properly Jewish "for the sake of political-legal security" (Fohrer, cited in Klein: 18). After Hitler's attempt to rid the earth of all Jews, Jews would not be moral unless they were concerned with the security of themselves and their children. Yet the anti-Jewish ideology requires its holders to view Israel merely as evidence of new failure on the part of the Jews.

Similarly, in two lectures on the conflict in the Middle East, a biblical theologian set forth the thesis that the settled condition of a nation in a particular country was never central to Israel; rather, Israel is called to fulfill the special ideal of freedom (Bartsch: 2). Establishment of the state of Israel contradicts the task of pro-claiming freedom. Hence, were Jews to repudiate ownership of Jerusalem, the city would "become the expression of the longing for freedom with which the Jewish people in the ghettos were filled" (Bartsch: 4). Clearly, in this writer's view, the ideal state of affairs for Jews occurred historically either during the wilderness wanderings or while victims confined to ghettos, since in these circumstances their longing for freedom could be most purely expressed.

These contemporary views are presented here to show that they are not much different from the classical *adversus Judaeos* ideology which assigned to the Jews the fate of wandering the earth, homelessly. However different their procedures, the conclusion is the same: Jews have no right to be safe and secure any-where. Indeed, such concerns are scorned as "typically human," and therefore matters with which Jews should, apparently, not be concerned. Aside from the obvious immorality of playing fast and loose with someone else's security, that such anti-Jewish ways of thinking should be articulated by Christians after Hitler's "final solution" is simply odious. Clearly, we must resolutely set aside the *adversus Judaeos* inheritance if we are to think responsibly about the land and state of Israel today.

A Theological Challenge

Among a growing number of Christian thinkers, Paul M. van Buren notes that the re-establishment of Israel as a Jewish state raises critical questions for traditional Christian theology. The church, claims van Buren, must recapture the Reformation ideal of itself as *semper reformanda*, always reforming, particularly in relation to the state of Israel. Two facts set a serious challenge before the church today: the establishment of the state of Israel and the growing recognition, prompted by the Second Vatican Council, "that the covenant between God and the Jewish people is eternal" (van Buren, 1987: 120). The reason these two facts place the church in a new situation is that "never in its history has it been confronted with Jewish sovereignty in its own land, and not since some time in the late first century has it acknowledged the Jewish people to be Israel in its enduring covenant with God" (van Buren, 1987: 120).

The reality of the state of Israel poses several questions for Christians. Chiefly, we are pressed to call into question how we understand Jewish scripture (the Prime Testament) and to deal with the continuing presence of Marcionism and Gnosticism in the church, i.e., with the excessive tendency to spiritualize historical reality. Also insistent are questions about the theological and moral significance of power and the meaning of God's covenant with Israel. To make a start on talking about Israel in a new way, we will consider the land of Israel in Jewish tradition.

The Jewish Land Tradition

Judaism's view of Israel as the "promised land" is a very different matter from Christian ideas of the "Holy Land." For Judaism, the land of Israel is of ultimate importance and value, a place central to the covenant between God and Israel. This land is a unifying theme in Israel's understanding of God as a God who is faithful to promises and Israel's understanding of itself as a people who have obligations to this gracious God.

Martin Buber, who staunchly stood for achieving "a lasting brotherly understanding with the Arabs in all areas of public life," eloquently expressed the Jewish land tradition (Buber: ix). It is Buber to whom we turn for a statement on the significance of Zion in Judaism, because Christians need to be aware that an authentic Zionist (which Buber was) must also stand for justice to all other inhabitants of the contemporary land of Israel. Buber's Zionism, he said, "turns with horror against the methods of a domineering nationalism" (Buber: x). Jews, who have experienced rejection in their life among the nations, cannot adopt similar attitudes toward Arabs, so Buber contended.

The land is a land of promise, which means that it is always to be understood as a gift from God to the people Israel; it "was at no time in the history of Israel simply the property of the people" (Buber: xix). Rather, it was both gift and command: command to make of it what God intended for it. As the story goes, we first meet the biblical land tradition in the creation story. From the beginning, the destiny of human beings is tied up with the soil and the fate of the soil is bound up with human beings. First, there was a fertile earth, an *Adama*, but no human beings, no *Adam*, to serve it. Then God creates human beings and puts them in the garden growing in the *Adama*. The human beings "and the earth are united one with the other from the beginning and to the very end of time" (Buber: 11).

Yet in the same story the human beings sin and God curses the earth, the *Adama*; people and the earth are bound up with one another for good or ill, but the earth's fate is determined by our conduct. Yet its fate is, in turn, our fate, a sobering thought in the ecological, nuclear age in which we live. When the earth is filled with our violence, it itself becomes corrupt (Genesis 6:11). The land itself and human beings live in responsible communion with one another. Our sin "bring[s] guilt upon the land" (Deuteronomy 24:4), and murder "pollutes" it (Numbers 35:33). The communion between people and the earth is of an ethical character (Buber: 13).

There are four major points in Buber's interpretation of the Jewish land tradition, which are to be taken in the context already introduced. First, all human dealings connected with the soil are to be engaged in honestly. Acquiring land and selling the harvest of the fields are to be done morally. Tracts of land are not to be endlessly added to one another, with the result that there is an ongoing disparity between the rich, who have land, and the poor, who do not. At the conclusion of his defense of his integrity, Job alludes to the unjust usurper of land who has caused the death of its owners, saying that the land cries out against him and its furrows weep (Job 31:38). Amos criticizes those who make excess profit on harvest and who "bring the poor of the land to an end," because they "deal deceitfully with false balances" (Amos 8:5). The land and Israel are partners with God in a moral covenant.

Second, the land that is given to Israel is to have "a sabbath of solemn rest" every seventh year (Leviticus 25:4), when fields cannot be sown or vineyards pruned. In an earlier version of this tradition (Exodus 23:10ff.), Israel's claim to the land is relaxed and its yield "made available to all the hungry" (Buber: 14). In the later, Levitical, version, the land receives a rest from work and celebrates a holiday dedicated to God. "The idea is that the earth is from time to time to be free, so as not to be subjected to the will of man, but left to its own nature, to be like a no-man's land" (Buber: 15). It is a reminder to Israel that the land, on which Israel merely sojourns, belongs to God (Leviticus 25:23). The Sabbath of the land shows that Israel's relation to the land must be one of responsible communion, that any idea of a reckless domination over the earth cannot be derived from the biblical tradition.

Third, the covenantal idea that the land of Israel is a gift from God does not mean that God gave a land only to one people. What it means is that from God's perspective, landlessness is bad; for a people, landlessness means exile, homelessness, and suffering. Landedness is necessary to living the kind of responsible life God wants for us. Other people, too, have their lands, even if they do not recognize that every land is a gift from God: "Did I not bring up Israel from the land of Egypt, and the Philistines from Caphtor and the Syrians from Kir?" (Amos 9:8). Thus God reminds Israel that God has also brought other peoples into their present domains.

Fourth, the land was promised to Abraham and his descendants for a purpose—so that "by you all the families of the earth shall bless themselves," i.e., "so that you will be a blessing" (Genesis 12:1-3). How is Israel to be a blessing? By living in *eretz Israel*, the land of Israel, a life based on God's *Torah*, God's teachings, a social-moral life that manifests the redemption of God in a liberated and restored human life. The people of Israel in the land of Israel is given and called to be the "herald and pioneer of the redeemed world" (Buber: 35). To live according to the way, *Torah*, of God, Israel must be able to do that somewhere, in some place. The land of Israel is that "storied place" in the biblical tradition.

A noted Christian scholar of the Hebrew scriptures shows Christians what we have overlooked in our reading of the Bible. According to him, the Bible is centrally "concerned with the issue of being displaced and yearning for a place" (Brueggemann: 2). By "land" the Bible means "*actual earthly turf* where people can be safe and secure, where meaning and well-being are enjoyed without measure or coercion" (Brueggemann: 2). Land is so central to biblical faith that biblical theology might well be organized around it as a theme. Land is place—not merely space, but space associated with historical meanings, storied space. The land of Israel is "*a place with Yahweh*, a place well filled with memories of life with him and promise to him and vows to him" (Brueggemann: 5).

Israel experienced landlessness as *sojourners* with Abraham on the way to an as yet nameless land, as *wanderers* with Moses on the way to the land of promise, and as *exiles* from Israel, dis-placed people. Yet having land "turned out to be nearly as great a problem and temptation as not having land" (Brueggemann: 9). Land brought kingship, and kings brought coercion, thus recreating the kind of social order from which Israel escaped in Egypt. "The very land that promised to create space for human joy and freedom became the very source of dehumanizing exploitation and oppression" (Brueggemann: 11). The land of promise became the land of problem. A grasping attitude toward land and its inhabitants renews the threat of landlessness, recalling the chaos of the wilderness, of the time when Israel was not yet a people.

Hence, for biblical Israel, land is both gift and temptation. Israel faces the options of accepting the land as gift or yielding to the temptation of so grasping the land as to reduce life in it to life without the God of Israel and without the obligations of the covenant (Brueggemann: 53). To Israel, land is both gift and responsibility. "Torah is Israel's way of living gifted life" (Brueggemann: 61). It is the way for Israel to enjoy the gift of land, the reminder to Israel of whose land it is and how it was given to Israel. Particularly the sabbath (rest) for the land recalls to Israel's awareness that land is a gift from God and that it is not fully given over to be exhausted for Israel's benefit. Also, *Torah* requires solidarity with Israel's brothers and sisters: with the poor, the stranger, the sojourner, the widow and orphan, with all those who are landless and therefore without status in the community.

Much interpretation of scripture has been informed by dichotomies between space and time, nature and history. In the Liberal and Neo-Orthodox Eras of theology, time and history were regarded as peculiarly Hebraic and Jews defined as a people of time, but not of space or place. Clearly, this will no longer do. There is no timeless space, no spaceless time, in the Bible or elsewhere; Israel's story is concerned with "storied place," a place redolent of memories of Israel's life with the God of Israel. Appreciation of the emphasis on land, which includes transmission of the inheritance of tradition from generation to generation, will also throw much light on the writings of the early church. The faithlessness of the prodigal son appears in a new perspective in relation to the theme of landedness and responsibility to the next generation, for example.

In Brueggemann's view, the biblical land tradition raises the possibility of new conversations between Christians and Jews today about Israel. The landedness/landlessness dialectic of scripture teaches all of us that "grasping for home leads to homelessness and risking homelessness yields the gift of home" (Brueggemann: 189). We long for home but live in ways that lead to homelessness. First, Christians will be unable to talk seriously with Jews until we recognize land as central to the agenda. The new conversation will never take place until Christians cease to misunderstand their faith in the kind of "spiritual" way that is alienated from concrete rootedness in a storied place.

While Arabs in Israel or the occupied territories clearly have rights, "the Jewish people are peculiarly the pained voice of the land in the history of humanity, grieved Rachel weeping" (Brueggemann: 190). Christians are hardly in a position to tell Jews what they should do, not since the painful history of Christian treatment of Jews has done so much to give shape to the present situation. But Christians could note "the dialectic of land and landlessness, that grasping leads to landlessness and gift [*Torah*] leads to home" (Brueggemann: 191). And they could point out, as do both Buber and Brueggemann, that the *Torah* is deeply concerned with the dispossessed, those without land, power, or voice, and can ask whether in Israel Arabs must not be included among the dispossessed.

A Short History of Ruling Powers

Because there is confusion as to who lost political control of what is now the state of Israel when it was created in 1948, a brief look at the record of ruling powers in the area is in order. From the century before the rise of the church until the fourth century, Rome controlled the area, and in the year 135 C.E. gave it the new name of Syria Palestina in honor of the Philistines, Israel's ancient enemies. With Rome's fall in the fourth century, the Byzantine Christian rulers of the eastern empire took control. In the seventh century, the year 632 C.E., the Arab Muslims took and held control of the land for four and a half centuries, locating their capital at Ramla (interestingly, not at Jerusalem). In 1099, Christian crusaders wrested control from the Arabs and held it until 1187, when the Mamelukes (non-Arab Muslims, chiefly Tartars, Mongols, and Kurds from Central Asia, former Arab slaves) came to power.

They remained in power until 1517, when the Ottoman Turks (also non-Arab Muslims) conquered the land. Israel was part of the Ottoman Empire for four hundred years, until the British captured the region in World War I, in 1917. Britain's control ended in 1947-48, when the United Nations voted to partition what was left of Palestine (after Churchill removed 80 percent of it and named it "Transjordan," today's Jordan). Says Barbara Tuchman, a widely read historian, "the territory never formed part of an Arab state in modern times [actually, not since 1099], having passed from Turkish sovereignty to the British Mandate" (Tuchman: 128).

Jewish Presence in Israel

It is well known that down through the centuries of dispersion from the land of Israel, Jews longed for Zion, ending every Passover with the statement "next year in Jerusalem." What is less well known is that there always were Jewish communities in Israel, A Jewish presence in the land, for the two millennia reaching from the Roman conquest to the birth of the state of Israel in 1948. Wrote James Parkes, a noted Christian scholar of relations between Christians and Jews: "The real title deeds were written by the . . . heroic endurance of those who had maintained a Jewish presence in the land through the centuries, in spite of every discouragement" (cited in Rudin: 17). By way of example, the tiny village of Peki'in in Galilee has existed continuously for 2,500 years, its recently restored synagogue having been built in the second century with stones brought from Jerusalem after the destruction of the temple (Rudin: 18).

As conditions grew increasingly worse for Jews in Europe, the Jewish population in Israel slowly enlarged. By the eleventh century, some fifty Jewish communities had come into being. As Jews were forcibly expelled from England, France, Geneva, Spain, Portugal, and the provinces of Germany, Jewish communities in Israel grew, although slowly, and sometimes Jews in the diaspora were able to send support to the Jews in Israel. Never has Israel been without a Jewish presence.

Israel Today

No other country faces as many urgent problems compressed into so small a space, under such imperative demands of time and heavy burden of history, as Israel. No bigger than Massachusetts, a state that needs only one telephone book, Israel must continue to create a national existence while dealing with the hostility of four neighboring states commonly committed to its destruction. Also, it must cope with the enduring legacy of the wars started against it—the fact that it has become an occupying power on the West Bank and the Gaza Strip. Exercising military control over increasingly rebellious people is a task that Israel does not need and that is no part of any appropriate Zionist philosophy.

Israel already has enough work to do: maintain constant military alertness in its state of siege, create a coherent people out of a highly diverse immigrant population, and run an economy capable of undergirding defense while absorbing a steady flow of newcomers. Military alertness is dictated by geography: no part of the country is out of range of contemporary weapons. To be independent in its food supply, it has to reclaim the desert and restore fertility to the soil; half the land requires irrigation, and the water supply is inadequate. Desalinization of sea water needs to be made economical, particularly in the southern desert. Nor can the burden of history be lifted: six million trees have been planted in the Judean hills as a "Forest of Martyrs," and at Yad Vashem, the national archive of the final solution, an avenue of trees in honor of the "Righteous Gentiles" who saved Jewish neighbors.

Meanwhile, Israel must deal with four distinct groups of Arabs. First are the roughly six hundred thousand Arabs who are full citizens of Israel; these are the Arabs who remained in Israel during the war of independence in 1948-49. Seventy-Eight percent of them are Sunni Muslims; 14 percent are Christians (Rudin: 51). Second are the one million plus Arabs who live in the West Bank (650,000) and on the Gaza Strip (363,000). Israel officially refers to these as "administered territories"; Arabs call them "occupied lands." Third are the one and a half million Palestinians residing in Jordan, Lebanon, Syria, Kuwait, Saudi Arabia, and Egypt. Only Jordan has made citizens of its Palestinian residents; the rest are held in a condition of statelessness.

Last, there are about 157 million Arabs living in the twenty-one states that are members of the Arab League. The policies and attitudes of these states toward Israel differ significantly from one another; Egypt has signed a peace treaty with Israel, while four states have remained officially in a state of war with Israel since 1948.

Criticism of Israel

Most criticism of Israel today focuses on its treatment of Palestinian Arabs in the Gaza Strip and the West Bank. Israeli Arabs are full citizens of Israel and have representatives in the Knesset. Palestinian refugees in Arab countries constitute what is probably the most easily solved refugee problem in the world;

those countries could integrate them into their populations, as Israel did with an equal number of Jewish refugees from Arab countries and as the United States has done with millions of people throughout its history. It is on the Palestinians in the West Bank and Gaza Strip that criticism concentrates. How should Christians talk of Israel critically?

Some theologians, taking this question seriously, have suggested some helpful ground rules in this regard. Robert McAfee Brown has proposed four. Recognizing the precariousness of Israel's existence, threatened as it is from so many directions, the *first* is that *"Christians must unequivocally affirm the right of Israel to exist and prosper"* (R.M. Brown: 338). Believing that Israel cannot be reduced to a pawn on a fundamentalist Christian eschatology, the *second* is that *"Christians must disavow Armaggeddon scenarios"* (R.M. Brown: 338); thus Christians should not affirm Israel's existence temporarily until the end of the world begins (no doubt soon) as a result of conflict in the Middle East. Third, because the "final solution" dare not be forgotten, Christians *"must understand why Jews equate the state of Israel's survival with Jewish survival"* (R.M. Brown: 338). And, because Jews are faced with a crushing weight of rejection of Israel, left to wonder why Israel might need *more* critics, Christians should *"understand why Jews of the diaspora are reluctant to criticize the state of Israel publicly"* (R.M. Brown: 338).

In the light of these ground rules for discussion, Brown makes three points. Christians, he claims, (1) should find it possible to "criticize this or that political action by the state of Israel without automatically being labeled anti-Semitic" (R.M. Brown: 339). When such name-calling does occur, Christians have a right to hear other Jewish voices raised in their defense. Jews need to understand (2) "that Christian disagreement with certain political policies of the state of Israel entails a theological as well as a political judgment" (R.M. Brown: 339). The theological judgment he has in mind is one which Christians have learned from Israel, that of idolatry or "giving uncritical allegiance to human constructs," the greatest candidate for which is always the state, which desires to be "placed above criticism" (R.M. Brown: 339). The point is not that Israel should be examined with a magnifying glass by Christians looking for something to criticize. Jews and Christians alike properly protest when this kind of double-standard test is applied to a nation. But the point is simply that criticism "of *every* nation . . . is a part of the prophetic tradition that Jews and Christians share" (R.M. Brown: 339).

Christians should be able to hear (3) Jews speaking critically of Israel's policies if injustice is being done. The prophetic tradition requires all of us to protest against injustice wherever it happens. It is a sign of great health both that considerable internal criticism within Israel has always been present, no less so today, and that such criticism also takes place in the diaspora, e.g., among American Jews.

In a courageous essay, Rabbi Dennis Sasso of Congregation Beth-El Zedeck in Indianapolis, does precisely this. Recognizing that the fault is as much that of Israel's neighbors as Israel's, he laments the fact that Israel has "run its affairs for the past twenty years as an occupationist state" (Sasso: 1). Sasso contends that such a state of affairs is not in Israel's best interests, that it is an economic drain on the state, that it contradicts her democratic self-understanding and threatens Israel's life with insecurity and the specter of civil war. He contends that negotations between Israel and Palestinians, including the PLO, can no longer be avoided (Sasso: 1). He argues that the army should be withdrawn from the camps and that the PLO must recognize Israel's right to exist. If that is not forthcoming, then Israel should unambiguously assert the rights of Palestinian statehood and put the burden "upon those who refuse to meet and negotiate with her" (Sasso: 2).

What is called for is an end both to the rejectionist stance of the Arab states and the terrorism of the PLO, on the one hand, and the strong-headed policy of the current Israeli government on the other. The moral, prophetic point he eloquently makes is that a people schooled in homelessness, as Jews have been, cannot "advocate the homelessness of others—even our enemies" (Sasso: 2). Rabbi Sasso's concerns are hardly unique among American Jews; indeed, they express the frustration with Israeli policy felt by many.

When Christians feel they must criticize Israel, they should take care, in the light of Brown's eminently sensible ground rules, not to speak in such a way that their words could bring aid and comfort to those who deny Israel's right to exist and prosper. Christians already carry enough moral scars from the history of

Christian talk about and treatment of Jews to add any more disfiguring marks to the Christian countenance.

What do Jews have a right to expect Christians to do with regard to criticism of Israel? First, they have a right to expect Christians to remember that prophetic criticism is always self-criticism. Christians who are uncritical of the anti-Judaism of the Christian tradition are unable to criticize Israel "prophetically," because they fail to realize that criticism, like charity, begins at home. Second, Jews have a right to expect Christians to remember that prophetic criticism is always a criticism of what one loves. Christians who have never expressed or acted out their love for Jews and Israel can hardly expect to be taken seriously when they decide to criticize either one. Third, Jews have a right to expect Christians to remember that moral judgments are always universal in character. When Israel regularly comes in for criticism from the church or ecumenical bodies, and those groups never criticize Christian anti-Judaism or the treatment of Soviet Jews, the prophetic church loses moral credibility. Fourth, as I hope was made clear in the earlier part of this chapter, there is much that Christians can learn about the nature of biblical faith in a conversation with Jews about Israel. When it comes to criticism, it is at least as blessed to receive as it is to give.

7

Jewish Holidays and Spirituality

The Mending of the World

In this chapter we will look at the other side of Jewish piety, that dealing with worship, holidays, and spirituality. It is the "other" side, because the focus here is not on instruction as *halakah* or way of life but on piety and worship. Yet piety is not separate from the stress on Judaism as a way of life consisting of good deeds (*mitzvot*) and guided by practical moral reason (*halakah*). Instead, worship, prayer, and spirituality, in Judaism, are the other side *of the same coin.*

Judaism has always held that the world is in need of redemption and that, by God's grace and human deeds, it is redeemable. In the aftermath of the Hitler era, some Jewish thinkers have reappropriated a medieval idea that, as the world was being created, some of the vessels containing the creative light of God collapsed under the strain and broke. As a result, the world is in urgent need of mending (*tikkun*). All individuals have their allotted tasks of mending, the sparks of God's light that only we can liberate. We contribute to mending the world by doing *mitzvot.* Our task is to join God in mending and liberating the world.

The most straightforward way to define a *mitzvah* (*mitzvot* = plural) is to say that a *mitzvah* is anything that dignifies or enhances life. Enjoying any intimate pleasure, for example, is a *mitzvah.* Any act of kindness or generosity, any support for a deserving cause, is a *mitzvah.* The range of *mitzvot* is as wide as life itself. It

102

is a *mitzvah* to keep one's body clean, to visit the sick, to teach, to provide an honest service or product, to employ someone in useful work. One may never treat other people as instruments, nor injure, oppress, or humiliate them. We may not deceive or lie to or about people, because misused words can be as destructive as any weapon.

Righteous conduct is not a matter of unusual courage or brave acts. It has more to do with the day-to-day practice of good deeds, the ordinary healthy acts and questioning of evil and injustice, which if done regularly will not put us in a situation in which only heroes can act. Righteous conduct includes charity, but in the Jewish view focuses more on the justice that tries to prevent charity by preventing poverty. It is more moral to eliminate poverty than to be charitable to the poor. The *mitzvah* system of Judaism prohibits allowing property rights ever to take precedence over basic human needs, and declares that peace (*shalom*) is the highest of all moral concerns.

While the stress here is on the moral *mitzvot*, not all *mitzvot* are moral. Of the 613 commandments that the Jewish tradition finds in the *Torah*, two-thirds pertain to agriculture in the state of Israel, and of the remainder the majority are ritual *mitzvot*. The commandment to remember the Sabbath day and keep it holy (Exodus 20:8) is the chief example of a ritual *mitzvah*. While in theory all commandments are of equal weight, should there be a conflict between an ethical and a ritual commandment, one should choose to observe the ethical commandment. Any commandment may be violated if it conflicts with saving a life. The picture in the gospels of Jews as more concerned with ritual purity than moral acting is a caricature.

So Many Commandments?

Christians are familiar with Jesus' summary of all the commandments into the "great commandment" of love of God and of the neighbor (Mark 12:28-31). Because we are accustomed to dealing with the commandments in summary form, we are likely to be puzzled by the very number of commandments in Judaism. Why so many? The answer is basically two-fold. First, the commandments in the Prime Testament cover the whole life of a people, a society, and a state. Loving the neighbor is a nice idea, but it does not tell one what to do in particular, let alone difficult, situations. There are so many commandments because, for example, if one understands what it means to love one's neighbor, then one will not drive a car while under the influence of alcohol. Second, not only must abstract generalities be made concrete and specific, but because times change specific commandments must be updated.

Nonetheless, in his summary of all the commandments into two, Jesus was following a well-established Jewish practice at his time. The story is told of Hillel, a contemporary of Jesus, that a Gentile asked him to "teach me the whole law while standing on one foot." Hillel's response was: "What is hateful to you do not to your fellow: that is the whole law; all the rest is explanation; go and learn" (Montefiore: 200). Another Jewish contemporary of Jesus, Philo of Alexandria, distinguished between "two fundamental teachings to which numberless individual teachings and statements are subordinated: in reference to God the commandment of honoring God and piety, in reference to humanity that of the love of humanity and justice" (Swidler: 106). The most colorful rabbinic account of the summary of the commandments is the one which tells us that David in Psalm 15 reduced the 613 commandments to eleven; followed by Isaiah, who reduced them to six (Isaiah 33:15); followed by Micah, who reduced them to two ("do justice and love kindness and walk humbly with your God" —Micah 6:8); followed by Habakkuk (2:4), who reduced them to one, saying: "the righteous shall live by his faith" (Montefiore: 199).

Motivation and the Love of God

In spite of what was said in the first chapter about the relation between grace and *Torah*, Christians might nonetheless harbor the suspicion that post-biblical Judaism is a works-righteous religion. This is not the case; what is more likely is that only in a morally serious faith can God's grace and forgiveness be adequately appreciated. The first way in which we see this in Judaism is the importance laid on the intention (*kavvanah*) with which an act is done. *Kavvanah* is the antidote to a mechanical keeping of the commandments (Lange: 37). Said an ancient rabbi: "It matters not whether you do much or little, so long as your heart is directed to heaven [God]" (Montefiore: 272).

Intention is also related to the mercy of God, as is reflected in the rabbinic comment that if we decide to give alms to the poor and do so, God rewards us; if we decide to give and then discover that we have no money, God rewards us exactly as if we had given; if we neither give nor ask others to give but are kind to the poor in words, God still rewards us (Montefiore: 275). "Rewards" here are not evidence of works-righteousness. Indeed, in the comment related above God rewards in the absence of any work. Intention makes all the difference in Jewish observance; having the right intention while failing to carry out a commandment suffices, while carrying out the commandment without the right intention does not.

It is similar with our love of God, *lishmah*. To do something with *lishmah* is to do it for its own sake. To study *Torah* for the love of God is one thing; to study it out of an ulterior motive, such as to become rich, or be called "Rabbi," or to receive a reward, is another. The former is a law of love; the latter is a law without love (Montefiore: 277). This is what was meant by the saying that we "must not make the words of the *Torah* an ax to cut with, or a garland" with which to crown ourselves (Montefiore: 278). Rabbi Machman ben Isaac went so far as to say: "Better is a sin which is done *lishmah* than a commandment which is not done *lishmah*" (Montefiore: 279). Another implication of *lishmah* is that God prefers us to love both Godself and our fellow human beings, but failing that, it is better to love people and not God than to love God and not people.

Grace and Good Deeds

Christians who understand their faith appropriately know that it is God's grace freely given to them (as to all others) that enables and empowers them to love their neighbors as themselves and to work for their liberation from any and all forms of oppression. Jews, too, are aware of the priority of God's grace; one reason why they think it should be easy for us to do good is that we have assistance from God in doing so. Rabbi Berechiah told the fanciful story that as God was about to create human beings, God foresaw that the result would be a mixture of good and evil. God was faced with a dilemma: "If I create him, wicked beings will issue from him; if I do not create him, how can the righteous issue

105

from him?" What did God do? God removed the wicked from God's sight and created human beings out of mercy (Montefiore: 88).

God commands us to do justice, but beyond human deeds lie God's compassion and grace. To repent in Judaism, all we have to do is to "turn" to God with the slightest indication of genuine repentance and we will find God ever ready to listen to the cry of God's creatures in their distress. Reminiscent of some of the stories of Jesus about God's mercy is the comment on Psalm 55:22, which lays out the difference between God and a human protector; the latter, having been petitioned several times by one seeking protection, "turns from him altogether. But God is not thus; whenever you worry Him, He receives you" (Montefiore: 88).

Jewish piety and spirituality, therefore, are radically oriented to this world and to its mending by the good deeds that only human beings can do. Yet it is also keenly aware of human frailty and failure, of our need for God's forgiveness, as it is also aware that the God who lays upon us a unique commandment—that we love all our neighbors as we love ourselves—is also the God of a unique promise—that we are graciously loved by God. It is God's steadfast love that empowers our activity.

The Sabbath

In Christianity, one dimension of meaning of the Lord's Supper is that it is a "foretaste of things to come." It is an eschatological feast in the midst of time and history, an indication of what things will be like when all human beings can sit at table, in peace with one another and in the presence of God. Also, the ideal situation in the church is that Christians get a weekly taste of this "appetizer" to the eschatological banquet. In Judaism, the Sabbath is the foretaste of things to come. Abraham Joshua Heschel remarks that the Jewish tradition provides no definition of eternity, but it does tell us "how to experience the taste of eternity or eternal life in time" (Heschel: 1951: 74). He relates the legend that

At the time when God was giving the Torah to Israel, He said to them: My children! If you accept the Torah and my mitzvot, I will give you for all eternity a thing most

106

precious that I have in my possession.

And what, asked Israel, is that precious thing which Thou wilt give us to obey Thy Torah?

The world to come.

Show us in the world an example of the world to come.

The Sabbath is an example of the world to come
(Heschel, 1951: 73).

The Sabbath is a weekly period of recreation and restoration, a day when work is prohibited, when we must loaf systematically. It is a reminder of the exodus from Egypt, a celebration of freedom. It is a day of rest for all—rich and poor, employers and employees, human beings and animals (farmers may not make their draft animals work). It is a time of joy and delight, when food, drink, song, and pleasant recreation are the object. The rabbis encouraged married couples to make love on the Sabbath and deemed it an added blessing to do so (Greenstein: 45). An extra candle is lighted at the Sabbath dinner, for the additional brightness of the day, and wine is used as a symbol of joy. The day is devoted to whatever activities, other than work, enhance and dignify life—worship, learning, reading, leisure, taking a walk, visiting the sick, taking a nap. Little wonder that in a typical Sabbath service in the synagogue, one hears the line: "More than Israel has kept the Sabbath, has the Sabbath kept Israel."

Leo Trepp recalls his experience in a Nazi concentration camp where there was no day of rest: "The toil was endless, the future hopeless; . . . soon we all ceased to think in human terms, and became merely vegetating beasts of burden, no longer living" (Trepp: 177). Judaism rescues humanity from this condition by giving it the Sabbath; the Sabbath is a Jewish invention. It has passed into Christianity, which observes it (more or less) on Sunday, and into Islam, which keeps it on Friday. Today, in American Christianity, "the Lord's day" is barely distinguishable from other days. In two-income families, it tends to be another day of work, in which we do the work that no longer gets done on the other days. A good way to reinvigorate one's own life and to develop a greater appreciation for Judaism would be to set aside again a day on which we can do nothing except loaf systematically.

Christians must wonder why the rabbis generated so many

laws or decisions surrounding the Sabbath, why so many kinds of work were prohibited. The answer lies in an insight once articulated by Joe Garagiola during a baseball telecast. Tony Kubeck had just said that a mutual friend had undergone minor surgery. Retorted Garagiola: "Minor surgery is surgery that someone else is having; if I'm having it, it's major surgery." Paraphrasing Garagiola's remark will help us understand Judaism's prohibitions on work: "If I'm doing it, it's work; if you're doing it, it's not."

Rest excludes work, but if what constitutes work is left to individual interpretation, the well-to-do might decide that the tasks of their employees are not work. So, the rabbis defined work in detail, hence the many prohibitions. Yet it is work that is prohibited, not joy; the Sabbath has about it none of the harshness that accompanied Sunday when I was a boy, when it seemed that the only thing I could not do was to have fun. Instead it is (and we Christians could learn something from this) "the jubilee of the whole world," a day that reveals the eschaton of time and space, a day when all life is redeemed from drudgery and becomes an end in itself in the presence of God.

The High Holy Days

In Judaism, days and seasons of the year are still oriented to the habits of ancient farmers in Israel. The day is over when work can no longer be done, and evening begins a new day. It is similar with the year, which ends when the crops have all been harvested; the new year begins in the fall, as does the Christian year with the first Sunday of Advent. In Christian history the new year has begun at various times—with Christmas on December 25, with Annunciation Day on March 25, and on Easter, which, since it is a movable day, must have been quite confusing. Our modern practice of beginning the new year on January 1 dates back only to 1582, when Pope Gregory XIII reformed the calendar (Boorstin: 598). Like Christians, Jews take note of New Year's Day on January 1 but do their serious religious business on a different calendar.

In the new year, which can begin any time between September 6 and October 4, the first ten days are called the "Ten Days of Remembrance." The closest Christian analogy to the High Holy Days is the season of Lent; both are solemn periods set

108

aside for self-appraisal and serious reflection. The Ten Days begin on *Rosh Hashanah*, the New Year, and terminate on *Yom Kippur*, the Day of Atonement. Traditionally, Judaism taught that every act of a person, good or bad, was registered by God in the book of life, and that the book was opened at the beginning of the new year for the inspection of every person's entries. Actions were weighed and measured, and a verdict reached and written down. But the judgment was not permanently sealed until *Yom Kippur*, leaving time for self-examination and resolve to change one's behavior in the coming year. The high holy days stress both the seriousness of sin and provide reassurance that God graciously forgives wrongdoing if we show signs of being serious about repentance.

New Year's Day, *Rosh Hashanah*, is distinguished by the blowing of a ram's horn, the *shofar*, reminding Jews of the serious personal self-examination demanded of them by the Days of Repentance. Yet, in the celebration at home, *Rosh Hashanah* is observed in a spirit of hope, accompanied by the *Kiddush*, the sanctification with wine, a reminder of joy for the new year, with a sweeter variety of the standard Sabbath bread, and with pieces of apple dipped in honey, indicating the hope that the year will be characterized by sweetness. Sin and repentance are serious matters, but God's grace is predominant.

The holiest day of the Jewish calendar is the Day of Atonement, *Yom Kippur*. It transcends in importance even the Sabbath, and the greeting Jews offer one another on it is: "May you be inscribed for a new year." A day of prayer, fasting, and self-examination, it is a time for Jews to concentrate on spiritual matters regarding the fasting that they undertake as making them more sensitive to the hardship suffered by oppressed peoples at the hands of oppressors. The liturgical color of the synagogue on *Yom Kippur* is white, symbolizing God's cleansing and forgiveness of the sinner: "Though your sins be as scarlet, they shall be white as snow" (Isaiah 1:18).

The Spirituality of Repentance

In a remarkable book on Jewish spirituality, David Blumenthal points out that after the sin of the golden calf, the *Torah* tells us that God taught Moses a prayer: "Lord, Lord—God Who loves compassionately and cherishes, Who is patient and over-flows with grace and truth. He stores up grace for thousands of generations. He forgives rebellious sin, purposeful sin, and inadvertent sin. He cleanses" (Exodus 34:5-7, Blumenthal's translation). Because God taught this prayer to Moses at the time of the greatest sin in Jewish history, it became central to Jewish liturgy; it is the refrain of the liturgy on the high holy days.

Speaking of God as loving, cherishing, being patient, and granting grace, the prayer teaches us of God's four different kinds of love. Stating that God "'overflows with grace' is to say that God loves us irrespective of our merits" (Blumenthal: 177). This is God's unconditional love, the love that comes from God because God *is* grace. Christians call it God's *agape*, God's all-inclusive love. However, when the prayer says that God "loves compassionately," it claims that God anguishes over our suffering, that God feels for us, that God is "internally affected" by us (Blumenthal: 177). Love here is empathy and is what Christians refer to as God's suffering love.

To say that God "cherishes" us is to affirm that because God likes us we are valuable, that we have "found favor" in God's eyes, as children "find favor" in the eyes of parents. This is God's parental love. It implies that God is really related to us, but it is not unconditional or compassionate love; it is the love that nurtures, treasures, and holds dear. It is the kind of love of which Christians speak when they use the metaphor of God as a shepherd, holding the sheep in God's arms.

Finally, to say that God is "patient" asserts that God "knows" us, that God "studies our ways" and "does not choose to judge us only on the basis of our manifest being," but accepts us for what we are, in spite of ourselves (Blumenthal: 178). This is the kind of love of which Christians speak when they say that God justifies us in spite of the fact that we remain sinners, that we are, as Luther often said, *simul iustus et peccator*, at one and the same time justified and sinful.

The season of repentance in Jewish spirituality should bring participants to the realization that God loves us, each and all, in grace, in compassion, in cherishing, and in patience. Also, the four types of God's love should make us aware that "God has a moral claim on our compassionate love, a right to our empathy," that the only proper response to God's love is to love God and the neighbor in return.

The Major Pilgrim Festivals

The calendar of the religious year in Judaism incorporates three major festivals. In their origins, they occurred at the end of different harvest periods and were agricultural celebrations; in the history of Israel their meaning was associated with a turning point in Jewish history. The first, *Sukkoth* (The Feast of Tabernacles or Booths), came to commemorate the period of wilderness wandering; the second, *Pesach* (Passover), celebrates the emancipation from Egyptian slavery; and the third, *Shavuoth* (Pentecost), solemnizes the revelation of God to Israel at Sinai. They are "pilgrim festivals," because in biblical times it was customary to make a pilgrimage to the temple in Jerusalem to give thanks for God's blessings.

The Feast of Tabernacles: *Sukkoth*

In our neighborhood in Indianapolis, we can always tell when *Sukkoth* is being observed. An Orthodox Jewish family living nearby builds a fragile, temporary hut (*sukkah*) on the lawn; the roof is made of branches, open to the sky. The hut is decorated with flowers, and the family takes its meals in the hut. It is a remarkable display of trust in other people, in a city where meals are usually eaten behind locked doors. At *Sukkoth* Jews step out of the protection of the home, place themselves beneath the starry sky, and feel perfectly protected, because God is their guardian. The frail hut commemorates the shelters Jews used during the period of wilderness wandering, the kind that is easily collapsible and easily put up again.

An alternative interpretation of the meaning of *sukkah* is that this unstable structure, open to the weather, reminds well-to-do Jews of the adversity suffered by the homeless and poverty stricken, who have to make do with such shelter as they can improvise. It is also a reminder of the impermanence of the treasures we can lay up for ourselves on earth, that our only ultimate security is in God. Not all Jewish families, not even all Orthodox families, build a *sukkah*, but an increasing number of urban families find in the week-long festival of "living in booths" a way of renewing contact with the world of nature from which an increasingly urbanized and technological civilization has estranged them. As we become increasingly aware of the ecology of nature and the ecological crisis in which we live, *Sukkoth* is being reinterpreted as a "superb holiday of homage to the principle of ecology" (Greenstein: 51).

The other symbol of *Sukkoth* is a cluster of special plants brought to the synagogue and waved during the recital of the Psalms of Thanksgiving (Psalms 113-118). The cluster includes a citron, called the *ethrog*, and the *lulav*, comprised of a branch of date palm, myrtle, and willows. Together, they represent all the kinds of vegetation produced by the earth. The citron, having smell and taste, symbolizes Jews who both know Torah and perform good deeds; the palm, having taste but no smell, stands for Jews who know Torah but do not perform good deeds. The myrtle, having smell but no taste, stands for Jew who perform good deeds but do not know Torah, and the willow, having neither smell nor taste, represents Jews who neither perform good deeds nor know Torah. Yet all form one human family in which each is essential and none is expendable. The last day of the weeklong festival is a time of merrymaking and joyful abandon.

Simchat Torah

The final day of *Sukkoth* is *Simchat Torah*, the joy of Torah. On this day, the annual cycle of scripture readings from the first five books of scripture is completed and begun again. Before the reading, the Torah scrolls are taken from the ark and the congregation walks around the synagogue with them, singing and dancing. Children carrying flags escort the Torah; an elder of the congregation is named "Bridegroom of the Torah," and reads the final paragraph of Deuteronomy. A young married member reads the beginning portion, Genesis 1:1—2:4, the story of the creation before the fall.

In the Soviet Union there are no Jewish calendars, no Jewish schools; the teaching of Judaism, even to one's own children, is illegal; consequently, few Jews know much about Judaism. Yet on Simchat Torah, Jews crowd the streets around the synagogues, coming to celebrate and just be together. An American Jew who was caught up in one such celebration found a note had been slipped into his pocket: "*Am Yisrael chai*, the people Israel lives." In one of his stories, Elie Wiesel describes the celebration of *Simchat Torah* in a Nazi concentration camp where, lacking a copy of the Torah, Jews found a little boy who remembered the *Shema* ("Hear, O Israel, the Lord our God, the Lord is One"), and "lifted the boy from the ground and began dancing with him—as though *he* were the Torah. And all joined in, they all sang and danced and cried" (Blumenthal: 183).

The Spirituality of *Simchat Torah*

By the time the last day of *Sukkoth* is reached, Jews have been engaged in the high holy season for almost two months, have criticized themselves, repented of their sins, engaged in self-examination, and attempted to fulfill the commandments of God in love, throughout seeking a wholeness in their relationship with God. On *Simchat Torah*, reading the story of creation before the fall, Jews briefly and fragmentarily regain a sense of the innocence of Eden, undergo a moment of what Paul Tillich used to call "theonomy," a time when the human will and the divine will are, fleetingly, at one with each other. The interspersing of the dancing and reading of the creation story with one another facilitates the celebration of "this moment of Eden" (Blumenthal: 194). The long season that began in penitence ends. With Torah in the hand, thanksgiving in the heart, trusting in God's providence, Jews step forth in faith, knowing that God is for them and with them, "Emmanuel," as Christians have learned to say.

The Festival of *Pesach:* Passover

Passover is the second major festival in the Jewish calendar. Initially it was an agricultural festival on which the first grains of ripened barley were cut and offered at the Jerusalem temple as an act of thanksgiving. It became, however, the chief celebration of freedom, specifically from slavery in Egypt. It is similar to other freedom celebrations and has been referred to as the Independence Day of the Jewish people, with the exception, however, that it regards God as the author of all freedom. The focal note of

Passover is the claim that Jews were liberated from slavery not merely for their own benefit, but in order to promote freedom for everybody, everywhere. Hence, there is a sense of incompleteness about Passover until the time when all people are liberated from oppression, until, as Jews say, the days of the Messiah have come.

Unleavened bread—the *matzah*—is the central symbol of Passover. In the rush to leave Egypt and the haste of departure, the lengthy time necessary for bread to rise was not available. It was necessary to leave with unleavened bread, which is called both "the bread of affliction" and the "bread of freedom." The major celebration is the *seder*, which means "order" and refers to the order followed by the ritual meal that celebrates Passover. The order is spelled out in a guide, usually a booklet, called the *Haggadah*, the "story." The *seder* is structured around the drinking of four glasses of wine, with an extra glass set out for the prophet Elijah, who is awaited with his message of the ultimate liberation of all human beings from oppression.

Although it is observed in the synagogue for single individuals, the *seder* is essentially a family occasion, celebrated at home. The sprig of parsley dipped in salt water is reminiscent of the tears shed in slavery (and also of the tears shed and loss suffered in the final solution). The order is intentionally planned to engage and sustain the interest of children, and the *seder* meal is a wonderful example of religious education at its best. The youngest child asks four questions, and the dessert is hidden away, with a prize offered the child who finds it. The message of Passover is one of liberation for all peoples from all forms of oppression. In these days when liberation theology is so important in Christian circles, Christian appreciation of the Jewish rootedness of our concern with liberation should become greater.

The Spirituality of Passover

The story of Israel's liberation from Egypt has its underside, the story of Egyptians upon whom were visited the plagues and who died in the sea after the Israelites had crossed it. In the Passover *Haggadah* this underside of the liberation of Israel from servitude in Egypt is remembered. In the service, the leader reminds the participants of the plagues by pouring drops of wine as the plagues are named, commenting that the wine is not poured out of joy: "According to an ancient Jewish tradition, we express our compassion for the suffering of the Egyptians. Although they were enemies and tormentors, they were also children of God and fellow human beings." Passover spirituality is one that affirms the solidarity of all victims of oppression and of all human beings as being knit together by the love and justice of God.

The Feast of *Shavuoth:* Pentecost

Shavuoth is the Hebrew word for "weeks." The name is applied to this festival because it takes place seven weeks after Passover. It also originated as an agricultural festival, occurring in late spring, and was an occasion for making a pilgrimage to the temple. Its historical import has to do with the giving of the covenant, the commandments, at Sinai. Because of the importance of studying Torah, many congregations schedule their confirmation services close to *Shavuoth*, as well as *bar* and *bat mitzvah* services. A frequent feature of such services, in addition to the fact that they are led by young people who demonstrate their religious education, is that all of the living generations of the family will line up on the podium—grandparents, parents, and children—and the Torah scroll will be passed from generation to generation, signifying the "passing on" of the tradition in the family.

The Spirituality of Pentecost

In Judaism, one of the highest forms of worship, if not the highest, is study. Somewhere along the line, Christianity has lost this emphasis and needs desperately to recover it. The greatest compliment congregations can pay rabbis is to express pride in their scholarship. Study is a year-round, daily occupation for those who take it seriously, but at *Shavuoth* in particular it is emphasized. The spiritual commitment required by hard, grubby study, entails great humility and readiness for self-criticism. If Christians are to re-appropriate their own tradition of scholarship, and pastors to again become teachers of the faith, we need to develop a scholarly spirituality.

115

Minor Festivals

To Christians, the best known minor festival in Judaism is *Hanukkah*, occurring as it does in December. Its message is one of religious freedom and, after the Nazi era, one of resistance to assimilation, i.e., of a vigorous assertion of one's freedom. It commemorates the rededication of the Jerusalem temple after the Maccabees had liberated it from Greek-Syrian tyranny. *Hanukkah* lasts for eight days and is distinguished by the eight-branch candelabrum (with an additional branch for the candle from which the others are lighted). In America, the practice of exchanging gifts at *Hanukkah* has increased.

Purim, occurring in the spring, commemorates the first successful struggle for survival of the Jewish people. The Book of Esther is read on *Purim*, and the children in the synagogue are supplied with noise-makers, with which they raise a racket at every mention of the name of Haman, who sought to exterminate the Jews. Esther and Mordecai are the heroes of the story. One of the more popular Jewish holidays, the occasion usually has an atmosphere of revelry, with Esther and Mordecai being cheered on and Haman hissed.

Tu b'Shevat is Arbor Day and has become an ecological observance. In Israel where the desert has been made to bloom, it is an important day, but everywhere Jews are it is a time for planting trees and underlining human responsibility for the ecosphere in which they live.

Summer is marked by two days of mourning and fasting, commemorating the day when the walls of Jerusalem were scaled and regular worship in the temple was stopped. The last day is the saddest day of the year, *Tisha b'Ab*, the day on which the first and second temples were destroyed. Other tragedies in Jewish history are also commemorated on this day—the expulsion from Spain in 1492, pogroms in Russia, the *Kristalnacht*, the night of broken glass in Germany (November 9, 1938). It is bold so to put it, but one might say that *Tisha b'Ab* is to Jews what Good Friday is to Christians. The reason it is bold to say so is that Good Friday was for so long, and often still remains, an occasion for venting negative feelings toward Jews. Yet it may not be too much to hope that in their common protest against evil and suffering, Christians could find common ground with Jews for envisioning a different kind of future.

A new day in the Jewish calendar is *Yom Hashoah*, Holocaust Memorial Day, which usually falls in April between the anniversaries of the uprising in the Warsaw ghetto in 1942 and the start of Israel's war of independence in 1948. *Yom Hashoah* is accompanied by a second new day, *Yom Ha-atzmauth* (Israel Independence Day), celebrated as Independence Day by Jews around the world by way of affirming solidarity with the Jews of Israel and with Israel as critical to Jewish life in our time.

That we mention these two observances at the end of this book is fortuitous, because they represent the two climactic events of our time with which Christians are still trying to come to terms: Hitler's attempt to rid the world of all Jews, and the rebirth of the state of Israel. Both events force conscientious Christians to re-examine their traditions and assumptions and to begin to come to terms with the reality of the Jews as the people of God in new and more creative ways than we have ever previously manifested. The hope is that this book will contribute to such a beginning.

Works Consulted

Agus, Jacob
1975 "The Reform Movement," "The Orthodox Stream," "The Conservative Movement." In *Understanding American Judaism*, Vol. 2, ed. Jacob Neusner. New York: KTAV: 5-30; 107-130; 199-218.

Ambrose
1956 *Letters 40 and 41*. In *Early Latin Theology*, ed. S. L. Greenslade. The Library of Christian Classics. Philadelphia: Westminster Press: 229-250.

Aquinas, Thomas
1977 "On the Production of Woman." In *Women and Religion*, ed. Elizabeth Clark and Herbert Richardson. New York: Harper & Row, 78-101.

Augustine
1975 *Reply to Faustus*. In *Disputation and Dialogue*, ed. Frank E. Talmage. New York: KTAV: 28-32.

Barmen Declaration, The
1973 "The Barmen Declaration." In *Creeds of the Churches*, ed. John H. Leith. Atlanta: John Knox Press: 517-522.

Barnabas
1979 *The Epistle of Barnabas*. In *The Ante-Nicene Fathers*, Vol. I, ed. Alexander Roberts and James Donaldson. Grand Rapids: Eerdmans: 137-149.

Bartsch, Hans Werner
1970 "Die Bedeutung Jerusalems für das jüdische Volk und die Stadt unter Besatzung, Materialen zum Nahostkonflikt, 47." *Evangelischer Arbeitskreis Kirche und Israel in Hesse und Nassau.*

Beker, J. Christian
1980 *Paul the Apostle: The Triumph of God in Life and Thought*. Philadelphia: Fortress Press.

Bethge, Eberhard
1974 "Troubled Self-Interpretation and Uncertain Reception in the Church Struggle." In *The German Church Struggle and the Holocaust*, ed. Franklin H. Littell and Hubert G. Locke. Detroit: Wayne State University Press: 167-184.

Black, Matthew
1973 *Romans*. London: Marshall, Morgan, & Scott.

Blumenthal, David R.
1988 *God at the Center: Meditations on Jewish Spirituality*. San Francisco: Harper & Row.

Bokser, Ben Zion

1979 "Witness and Mission in Judaism." In *Issues in the Jewish-Christian Dialogue: Jewish Perspectives on Covenant, Mission, and Witness*, ed. Helga Croner and Leon Klenicki. New York: Paulist Press.

Boorstin, Daniel J.

1983 *The Discoverers*. New York: Random House.

Brown, Raymond E.

1966 *The Gospel According to John, Vol. 1*. The Anchor Bible. Garden City: Doubleday & Co.

1979 *The Community of the Beloved Disciple*. New York: Paulist Press.

Brown, Robert McAfee

1988 "Speaking About Israel: Some Ground Rules." *The Christian Century*, 105: 338-340.

Brueggemann, Walter

1977 *The Land: Place as Gift, Promise, and Challenge to Biblical Faith*. Philadelphia: Fortress Press.

Buber, Martin

1973 *In Zion: The History of an Idea*, trans. Stanley Godman. New York: Schocken Books.

Cargas, Harry

1981 *A Christian Response to the Holocaust*. Denver: Stonehenge Books.

Chrysostom, John

1978 *Homily I Against the Jews*. In *Jews and Christians in Antioch*, ed. Wayne A. Meeks and Robert L. Wilken. Missoula, MT: Society of Biblical Literature: 85-104.

Cobb, John B.

1982 *Beyond Dialogue: Toward A Mutual Transformation of Christianity and Buddhism*. Philadelphia: Fortress Press.

Cohen, Shaye

1987 *From the Maccabees to the Mishnah*. Philadelphia: Westminster Press.

Cope, Lamar

1986 *Faith for A New Day: The New View of the Gospel of John*. St. Louis: CBP Press.

Cunningham, Philip A.

1986 *Jewish Apostle to the Gentiles*. Mystic, CT: Twenty-Third Publications.

Davies, W. D.

1974 *The Gospel and the Land*. Berkeley: University of California Press.

Dawidowicz, Lucy S. (ed.)

1976 *A Holocaust Reader*. New York: Behrman House, Inc.

Donahue, John R.

1973 *Are You the Christ?* Missoula, MT: Society of Biblical Literature.

Eckardt, A. Roy

1986 *Jews and Christians: The Contemporary Meeting*. Bloomington: Indiana University Press.

Elvira, Council of

1987 *Canons*. In *Morality and Ethics in Early Christianity*, ed. Jan L. Womer. Philadelphia: Fortress Press: 75-82.

Finkelstein, Louis
1970 *The Jews: Their History.* New York: Schocken Books.
Fisher, Eugene J.
1983 "The Impact of the Christian-Jewish Dialogue on Biblical Studies." In *Christianity and Judaism: The Deepening Dialogue,* ed. Richard W. Rousseau, S.J. Scranton, PA: Ridge Row Press: 117-138.
Friedlander, Albert H.
1985 "Tillich and Jewish Thought." In *The Thought of Paul Tillich,* ed. James Luther Adams, Wilhelm Pauck, and Roger L. Shinn. San Francisco: Harper & Row: 175-196.
Gaston, Lloyd
1987 *Paul and the Torah.* Vancouver, BC: University of British Columbia Press.
Glock, Charles Y. and Rodney Stark
1966 *Christian Beliefs and Anti-Semitism.* New York: Harper & Row.
Greenstein, Howard R.
1983: *Judaism: An Eternal Covenant.* Philadelphia: Fortress Press.
Heschel, Abraham J.
1951 *The Sabbath: Its Meaning for Modern Man.* New York: Farrar, Straus and Giroux.
1962 *The Prophets: An Introduction.* Vol. 1. New York: Harper & Row.
Hilberg, Raul
1979 *The Destruction of the European Jews.* New York: Harper & Row.
Himmelfarb, Milton
1987 "Jewish Perceptions of the New Assertiveness of Religion in American Life." *The Jews in Unsecular America,* ed. Richard John Neuhaus. Grand Rapids: Eerdmans Publishing Co.: 1-7.
Holmgren, Frederick
1979 *The God Who Cares: A Christian Looks at Judaism.* Atlanta: John Knox Press.
Hummel, Horace D.
1974 "Law and Grace in Judaism and Lutheranism." In *Speaking of God Today: Jews and Lutherans in Conversation,* ed. Paul D. Opsahl and Marc H. Tanenbaum. Philadelphia: Fortress Press: 15-30.
Irenaeus
1979 *Against Heresies.* In *Ante-Nicene Fathers,* Vol. I, ed. Alexander Roberts and James Donaldson. Grand Rapids: Eerdmans Publishing Co.: 315-567.
Jeremias, Joachim
1967 *Jerusalem in the Time of Jesus,* trans. F.H. and C.H. Cave. Philadelphia; Fortress Press.
1971 *New Testament Theology: The Proclamation of Jesus,* trans. John Bowden. New York: Charles Scribner's Sons.
Justin Martyr
1979 *The First Apology* and *Dialogue with Trypho the Jew.* In *The Ante-Nicene Fathers,* Vol. I, ed. Alexander Roberts and James Donaldson. Grand Rapids: Eeerdmans Publishing Co.: 163-187; 194-270.

Kee, Howard Clark

1977 *Community of the New Age: Studies in Mark's Gospel*. Philadelphia: Westminster Press.

Klassen, William

1966 *The Forgiving Community*. Philadelphia: Westminster Press.

Klein, Charlotte

1978 *Anti-Judaism in Christian Theology*, trans. Edward Quinn. Philadelphia: Fortress Press.

Knight, George A. F.

1962 *Law and Grace: Must A Christian Keep the Law of Moses?* Philadelphia: Westminster Press.

Kraemer, Heinrich and Jakob Sprenger

1977 *The Hammer Against the Witches*. In *Women and Religion*, ed. Elizabeth Clark and Herbert Richardson. New York: Harper & Row: 121-130.

Lacocque, Andre

1980 "The 'Old Testament' in the Protestant Tradition." In *Biblical Studies: Meeting Ground of Jews and Christians*, ed. Laurence Broadt, C.S.P., Helga Croner, and Leon Klenicki. New York: Paulist Press.

Lange, Nicholas de

1986 *Judaism*. Oxford: Oxford University Press.

Levenson, Jon D.

1985 *Sinai & Zion: An Entry into the Jewish Bible*. San Francisco: Harper & Row.

Luther, Martin

1975 *That Jesus Was Born a Jew* and *Concerning the Jews and Their Lies*. In *Disputation and Dialogue*, ed. Frank E. Talmage. New York: KTAV: 33-34; 34-36.

Melito of Sardis

1976 *Sermon "On the Passover,"* trans. Richard C. White. Lexington, KY: Lexington Theological Seminary Library.

Montefiore, C.G. and H. Loewe (eds)

1974 *A Rabbinic Anthology*. New York: Schocken Books.

Moore, George Foot

1921 "Christian Writers on Judaism." *Harvard Theological Review*, 14: 197-254.

Myers, J.M.

1975 *Grace and Torah*. Philadelphia: Fortress Press.

Neusner, Jacob

1973 *From Politics to Piety: The Emergence of Pharisaic Judaism*. Englewood Cliffs, NJ: Prentice-Hall, Inc.

Origen

1979 *Against Celsus*. In *Ante-Nicene Fathers*. Vol. IV, ed. Alexander Roberts and James Donaldson. Grand Rapids: Eerdmans Publishing Co.: 395-669.

Osborn, Ronald E.

1978 *Experiment in Liberty*. St. Louis: Bethany Press.

Parkes, James

1977 *The Conflict of the Church and Synagogue*. New York: Atheneum.

Pawlikowski, John T.
1976 *Sinai and Calvary.* Beverly Hills, CA: Benziger, Bruce & Glencoe, Inc.
Perrin, Norman
1974 *The New Testament: An Introduction.* New York: Harcourt Brace Jovanovich, Inc.
Pherigo, Lindsey P.
1971 "The Gospel According to Mark." In *The Interpreter's One-Volume Commentary On the Bible*, ed. Charles M. Laymon. Nashville: Abingdon Press: 644-671.
Plaskow, Judith
1978 "Christian Feminism and Anti-Judaism." *Cross Currents*, XXVIII: 306-309.
Rahner, Karl
1967 *Spiritual Exercises.* London: Sheed & Ward.
Raphael, Marc Lee
1984 *Profiles in American Judaism.* San Francisco: Harper & Row.
Rhoads, David
1982 "Narrative Criticism and the Gospel of Mark." *Journal of the American Academy of Religion*, L:411-434.
Richardson, Alan
1950 *A Theological Dictionary of the Bible.* New York: Macmillan.
Rivkin, Ellis
1984 *What Crucified Jesus?* Nashville: Abingdon Press.
Roth, Cecil
1970 *A History of the Jews.* New York: Schocken Books.
Rubenstein, Richard L. and John K. Roth
1987 *Approaches to Auschwitz: The Holocaust and Its Legacy.* Atlanta: John Knox Press.
Rudin, A. James
1983 *Israel for Christians.* Philadelphia: Fortress Press.
Reuther, Rosemary
1974 *Faith and Fratricide.* New York: Seabury Press.
Sanders, E.P.
1977 *Paul and Palestinian Judaism: A Comparison of Patterns of Religion.* Philadelphia: Fortress Press.
1983 *Paul, the Law, and the Jewish People.* Philadelphia: Fortress Press.
1985 *Jesus and Judaism.* Philadelphia: Fortress Press.
Sanders, Jack T.
1987 *The Jews in Luke-Acts.* London: SCM Press, Ltd.
Sanders, James A.
1983 "Canon and Calendar: An American Alternative Lectionary Proposal." In *Social Themes of the Christian Year*, ed. Dieter T. Hessel. Philadelphia; The Geneva Press: 257-263.
Sandmel, Samuel
1978 *Judaism and Christian Beginnings.* New York: Oxford University Press.
Sarna, Jonathan D.
1987 "Christian America or Secular America? The Church-State Dilemma of

American Jews." In *Jews in Unsecular America* ed. Richard John Neuhaus. Grand Rapids: Eerdmans Publishing Co.: 8-19

Sasso, Dennis C.

1988 "History Moves Forward." *Beth-El Bessamim*, February 15: 1-2.

Schoeps, H.J.

1961 *Paul: The Theology of the Apostle in the Light of Jewish Religious History*. Philadelphia: Westminster Press.

Schurer, Emil

1961 *A History of the Jewish People in the Time of Jesus*, ed. N. Glazer. New
York: Schocken Books.

Slingerland, Dixon

1986 "'The Jews' in the Pauline Portion of Acts." *Journal of the American
Academy of Religion*, LIV: 305-321.

Sloyan, Gerard

1983 *Jesus In Focus: A Life in Its Setting*. Mystic, CT: Twenty-Third
Publications.

Sobrino, Jon

1978 *Christology at the Crossroads*, trans. John Drury. Maryknoll, NY: Orbis
Books.

Stallsworth, Paul T.

1987 "The Story of an Encounter." In *Jews In Unsecular America*, ed Richard
John Neuhaus. Grand Rapids: Eerdmans Publishing Co.: 61-117.

Stendahl, Krister

1968 *The School of St. Matthew*. Philadelphia: Fortress Press.

Swidler, Leonard

1981 "The Jewishness of Jesus; Some Religious Implications for Christians."
Journal of Ecumenical Studies, 18: 104-113.

Tertullian

1979 *An Answer to the Jews*. In *Ante-Nicene Fathers*, Vol. III, ed. Alexander
Roberts and James Donaldson. Grand Rapids: Eerdmans: 151-173.

Tillich, Paul

1968 *A History of Christian Thought*, ed. Carl E. Braaten. New York: Harper
& Row.

Townsend, John T.

1979 "The Gospel of John and the Jews." In *Anti-Semitism and the Founda-
tions of Christianity*, ed. Alan Davies. New York: Paulist Press: 72-97.

Tracy, David

1982 "Religious Values After the Holocaust: A Catholic View." In *Jews and
Christians After the Holocaust*, ed. A. Peck. Philadelphia: Fortress Press.

Trepp, Leo

1973 *A History of the Jewish Experience: Eternal Faith, Eternal People*. New
York: Behrman House, Inc.

Tuchman, Barbara

1981 *Practicing History: Selected Essays*. New York: Alfred A. Knopf.

van Buren, Paul M.

1980 *Discerning the Way: A Theology of the Jewish Christian Reality*. New
York: The Seabury Press.

1987 "Ecclesia Semper Reformanda: The Challenge of Israel." In *Faith and Freedom: A Tribute to Franklin Littell*, ed. Richard Leibowitz. Oxford: Pergamon Press.

von Rad, Gerhard
1959 *Moses*. New York: Association Press.

Watson, Francis
1986 *Paul, Judaism and the Gentiles*. Cambridge: Cambridge University Press.

Waxman, Mordecai
1975 "The Ideology of the Conservative Movement." In *Understanding American Judaism*, Vol. 2, ed. Jacob Neusner. New York: KTAV: 247-257.

Williamson, Clark M.
1982 *Has God Rejected His People? Anti-Judaism in the Christian Church*. Nashville: Abingdon Press.
1987 "Postwar Reflections on the Holocaust From A Christian Point of View." In *Movements and Issues in World Religions*, ed. Charles Wei-hsun Fu and Gerhard Spiegler. New York: Greenwood Press: 515-539

Winter, Paul
1961 *On the Trial of Jesus*. Berlin: Gruyter & Co.

Notes

DATE DUE

AUG 07 1998			

The Plough Inn, Clifton Hampden, Oxon, has an ancient crutched foundation.

The Old Albion, Crantock, Cornwall, is four hundred years old.

*within God's house and to defile it with
scandalous games and lewd discourse . . . '*

A century after the Norman invasion, during
the Plantagenet rule of Henry II the first
national tax on ale was levied. A year later
in 1189 the City Council of London, in
common with other local governments of the
day, made a ruling *'that all ale-houses be
forbidden except those which shall be licensed
by the Common Council of the City at
Guildhall, excepting those belonging to persons
who build of stone, that the city may be secure'*.

Throughout the Middle Ages it was the
Church that provided for the needs of
travellers, both temporal and spiritual.
Although guests were not expected to pay
for a night's lodging, it was considered
reasonable that those who could afford to
make a contribution should so do. The
parsimonious King John spent some time at
Bury St. Edmunds and the prior gloomily
wrote in his journal, *'He availed himself of
the hospitality of St. Edmunds which was
attended with enormous expense, and upon
his departure bestowed nothing upon the Saint,
save thirteen pence sterling which he offered at
Mass'*.

As travel increased throughout the realm
it became exceedingly difficult for even the
larger religious establishments to cater for
the many guests requesting accommodation
and food. The responsibility was gradually
transferred to commercially operated
hostelries, although this did not mean that
the monasteries were relinquished from the
responsibility of brewing.

Rose & Crown,
Stratford-upon-Avon, Warws.

The Old Wellington Inn,
Manchester, Lancs.
This inn is one of the oldest
surviving buildings in the city.

The despotic reign of King John had been curtailed in 1215 by the signing of the Magna Carta and England was able to settle down to relative peace and tranquillity on the home front. The first major act of parliament affecting the trade of ale was legislated in 1267 by Henry III and became known as the Assize of Bread and Ale which was to result in the prices of these two essential commodities being controlled for the next three hundred years. A proclamation to the City of Bristol stated:

'It is forbidden by the King's writ that any brewer in the town of Bristol or in the suburbs of the same town, or any other vending ale there or elsewhere in the Kingdom of England, shall sell a gallon of the better ale for more than three halfpence, and of the weaker ale for a penny'.

The document went on to say that anyone who was indicted for an offence would be severely punished. An additional act of 1285 to regulate the prices of wines threatened, *' . . . and if the taverners exceed, their doors shall be shut'.*

The inns of Chaucer's time were far from luxurious and many of the pilgrims journeying to either Canterbury or Walsingham had to spend the night packed into large dormitories. Other wayfarers who were perhaps of more lowly station were accommodated in the guest houses of some of the monasteries. The worldly monks were able to live a life of ease and sauntering comfort, occasionally giving alms to the poor and showing lavish hospitality towards those who could afford to dine at the Abbot's table.

The New Inn at Gloucester, built in 1457, is typical of many medieval inns to be found up and down the country. It was originally built as a pilgrims' hostel for those visiting the nearby shrine of Edward II who was brutally murdered at Berkeley Castle in 1327.

An inn that one immediately associates with the Crusades must be the Ye Olde Trip to Jerusalem, sheltered beneath the rock on which Nottingham Castle stands. It has brewed its own beer for centuries and is one of a number of inns claiming to be the oldest in the country.

Other possible candidates for this honour include Grantham's Angel & Royal where Richard III signed the death warrant of the Duke of Buckingham in 1493. Masonry in the cellar dates back to 1213, but the main structure is circa 1450.

Meanwhile, back at the inn, many of the supposed pilgrims were able to satisfy their temporal lusts in debauchery and the singing of obscene songs, although the Canterbury publicans were instructed only to admit *'such as be of good disposition and conversation'*.

The taverns certainly were hotbeds of mischief and the weary traveller would often find himself surrounded by a host of thieves and scoundrels eager to rob him of whatever valuables he possessed. The inn, being the natural focal point of the community, attracted a cross section of society and it would have been possible to find a variety of fascinating people, minstrels, troubadours, sorcerers, gamblers, prostitutes and fraudulent rogues. Frequently the innkeepers were in league with robbers and after tipping them off about a likely victim, would expect to have a share of the takings.

The larger inns situated on important routes not only provided the traveller with food and rest but also stabling for horses. You could also expect to find a blacksmith in the vicinity, busily engaged at his forge.

In 1559, the young Queen Elizabeth is reported to have complained about the quality and price of beer. *'A kind of very strong bere calling the same doble-doble-bere which they do commonly utter and sell at a very grate and excessive pryce'*. She ordered that brewers must brew an equal amount of single beer and charge reasonable prices.

During one of the Queen's periodic country tours, one of many she was to make throughout her long reign, the Duke of Leicester wrote to her Lord High Treasurer,

Another ancient inn, The Fighting Cocks at St. Albans is an unusual octagonally-shaped building believed to date back to about 795 when it was built as a boat house to the ancient monastery. An underground passage once connected the inn to the monastery. Oliver Cromwell is said to have stayed there during the Civil War.

The Hoy and Helmet, South Benfleet, Essex.
A hoy was an East Anglian cargo sailing boat, named after its inventor. The helmet may refer to soldiers who were carried in such vessels during the Napoleonic Wars.

Burghley, and criticized the fact that *'There is not one drop of good drink here for her. We were fain to send to London and Kenilworth and divers other places where ale was; her own beer was so strong and there was no man able to drink it'.*

It hardly comes as a surprise to find that a number of our more senior inns played host to the first Queen Elizabeth at some time or another. It is quite possible that a few of the ascribed inns can be authenticated although it is certain that an equal number of claims are spurious.

The **King's Head** at Chigwell, Essex is a striking timbered coaching house, said to have been built during the reign of Henry VIII and it is believed that the Virgin Queen spent a night here during a hunting excursion. Legend said that an unfortunate page boy had his ears cuffed by Her Majesty for *'neglecting his duty'*.

Elizabethan England was truly a 'Golden Age'. The population of England and Wales numbered about 4,000,000, of whom four-fifths lived in rural parts. A census carried out in 1557 showed that there were 14,202 alehouses, 1,631 inns and 329 taverns in England and Wales and the number of licenses issued totalled 19,759.

A price list taken from Castle Combe in Wiltshire for that year indicates that there were at least three different types of ale available and the ale which had matured longer was the most expensive.

Best ale	per gallon	3d
Stale	,, ,,	4d
Second ale	,, ,,	1½d

This inn, The Sir John Barleycorn, near Ringwood in the New Forest, is named after a reputedly real person who, from time to time, has appeared in literature and has also been associated with beer and brewing.

Another New Forest pub, the Cat & Fiddle at Hinton Admiral has been named after the popular nursery rhyme.

The Talbot, Ledbury, Herefs. possesses a beautiful panelled room which dates from 1596.

| Stale | ,, | ,, | 2d |
| Smallest ale | ,, | ,, | $\frac{1}{2}$d |

Important towns like Reading could boast of as many as 3 taverns, 70 alehouses and 13 inns.

The Elizabethans were free from medieval superstition and expressed their enlightened love of life through music, wit and literature. Shakespeare was undoubtedly a frequent inhabitor of various inns and alehouses up and down the country. He must have certainly been known in the **Falcon,** just opposite where his house, New Place, stood in Stratford-upon-Avon. The Falcon has remained almost unchanged since then but it is not only in Stratford that we find Shakespearean links. He must have often crossed the Clopton Bridge to make the long and tiring journey south towards London.

Most of the taverns en route would have been familiar to him and in London he must have found time to visit many of the notable establishments of the day. The **Mermaid Tavern** which formerly stood in Cheapside was founded in 1603 by Ben Jonson and it is known that Shakespeare used to meet Jonson there. A bankside inn called the **Anchor** was close to the Globe Theatre and perhaps after an exasperating day of rehearsals Shakespeare might have been heard borrowing a line from one of his characters, Christopher Sly in the *Taming of the Shrew 'For God's sake, a pot of small ale'*.

The control and licensing of public houses during the 16th century was the responsibility of the local Justices of the Peace who were selected as residents of high standing and

The Falcon, Stratford-upon-Avon, Warws.

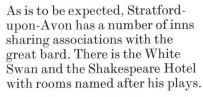

As is to be expected, Stratford-upon-Avon has a number of inns sharing associations with the great bard. There is the White Swan and the Shakespeare Hotel with rooms named after his plays.

The historic Shakespeare Hotel in Chapel Street, adjoining New Place.

endowed with considerable judicial and
administrative powers by the monarch. The
Church was still an important institution
and was reluctant to relinquish any of its
powers, particularly where the drinking
habits of the local populace were concerned.
Church wardens were empowered to break
into inns and interrupt the inhabitants,
forcibly carrying them off to church if the
question of sabbath day observance was
involved.

Not that the Church was beyond reproach.
The selling of church ales had long been a
lucrative source of extra income and Philip
Stubbs, writing in his *Anatomie of Abuses
1585* mentioned: *'The Churche Wardens . . .
of every parishe, with the consent of the whole
parishe, provide halfe a score or twentie
quarters of mault, . . . which mault beeying
made into very strong ale or beere, is sette to
sale, either in the churche or some other place
assigned to that purpose'*. He went on to say
how they amused themselves, *'swillying and
gullyng night and day, til they be as dronke
as rattes, and as blockishe as beastes'*. It was
not until 1595 that the selling of church ales
was finally prohibited in a decree signed by
the Lord Chief Justice in Bridgwater.

Harrison's *Description of England, 1577* has
left us an interesting contemporary account
concerning Elizabethan inns.
*'Those towns . . . have great and sumptuous
innes builded in them, for the receiving of such
travellers and strangers as passe to and fro.
. . . Every man may use his inne as his owne
house . . . and have for his monie how grate
or varietie of vittels, and what other service
himselfe shall think expedient to call for. Our*

The 16th century Feathers Hotel,
Ludlow, Salop.
 The iron-studded door
shows the arms of a number of
notable families.

Ye Olde Anchor Inn,
Upton-on-Severn, Worcs., is an
early 17th Century timber-framed
hostelry.

*innes are also very well furnished with
naperie, bedding, and tapisterie . . . for all
beside the linnen used at the tables, which is
commonlie washed dailie, is such and so much
as belongeth unto the estate of the ghest. Ech
comer is sure to lie in cleane sheets, wherein
no man hath beene lodged since they came from
the landress . . . '*

It all sounded extremely efficient and
comfortable. The integrity of the landlord
was also stressed and the guest assured that,
*'If he loose oughts whilest he abidest in the
inne, the host is bound by a generall custome
to restore the damage, so that there is no
greater securitie anie where for travellers than
in the greatest innes of England'.* However,
this was not always the case and it was
quite possible for the innkeeper to be in
league with a highwayman, as even Harrison
had warned, *'Certes, I believe not that chapman
or traveller in England is robbed by the waie
without the knowledge of some of them; for when
he cometh into the inne and alighteth from his
horse, the hostler forthwith is verie busy to take
down his budget or capcase . . . which he peiseth
slilie in his hand to feel the weight thereof'.*

Obviously the innkeeper would ensure that
the reputation of the inn was not tarnished
and that outrages were not to be carried out
on the premises. Certainly the Queen's
Highway was not a safe place for the
unprotected traveller, as is seen from many
contemporary accounts. It is probable that
Shakespeare was the victim of a highwayman
on at least one occasion. Shakespeare himself
referred to the seamy side of inn life when
he wrote about the inn-yard at Rochester in
King Henry IV.

The picturesque New Inn at
Clovelly, Devon.

The Bear Inn, Woodstock, Oxon,
is believed to date back to 1237.
Much of the present structure is
16th century.

Hopcroft's Holt at Steeple Ashton, Oxfordshire is associated with the notorious highwayman Claude Duval, who, on one occasion is said to have robbed a couple of £400. Having the audacity to ask the lady to dance with him, he refunded £300 when she accepted his invitation. Duval was hanged in 1670 and when, several years later, the landlord and his wife were found mysteriously murdered it was said that his ghost had returned.

In many places the accommodation that inns offered was almost as primitive and unsavoury as the homes of the poor but they were always important social and cultural centres, providing relaxation and refreshment to a cross section of the population.

Many of the wealthy inhabitants would adjourn to the local tavern with their guests, where a greater selection of wines was often available than could be found in their own cellars.

Not only did the menfolk spend an evening enjoying themselves at the local tavern. There would be such amusements as eating, drinking, fiddling and drama and the perceptive Thomas Platter in *Travels in England* 1599 was able to observe: '*And what is particularly curious is that the women as well as the men, in fact more often than they, will frequent the taverns and ale-houses for enjoyment. They count it a great honour to be taken there and given wine with sugar to drink; and if only one woman is invited, then she will bring three or four other women along and they gaily toast each other; the*

In the Market Place at Bungay, Suffolk, stands the Three Tuns, and on the opposite side of the road, the King's Head.

The London Apprentice, Isleworth, Middlesex, near the quiet historic quay, is a popular resting place for tourists. It is said to have received its name from the apprentices of the Livery companies who used to row up river.

The Rising Sun, Coltishall, on the Norfolk Broads.

husband afterwards thanks him who has given his wife such pleasure, for they deem it a real kindness'.

It all sounded jolly good fun and presumably everyone was able to leave as the best of friends. Gallants who spent enjoyable evenings at taverns would often hire guides to carry ladies home with lanterns.

Perhaps it would be fitting to let Fynes Moryson sum up the character of the Elizabethan inn, as he wrote in his *Itinerary* 1617.

'The world affords not such innes as England hath, either for food and cheape entertainment after the guests' owne pleasure, or for humble attandance on passengers, yea, even in very poor villages. For as soon as a passenger comes to an inne, the servants run to him, and one takes his horse, and walks him till he be cold, then rubs him and gives him meate. . . . Another servant gives the passenger his private chamber, and kindles his fire: the third puls off his boots and makes them cleane. . . . And when he sits down at table, the host or hostess will accompany him or if they have many guests will at least visit him, taking it for courtesy to be bid sit down. While he eats, if he have company especially, he shall be offered music, which he may freely take or refuse. . . . A man cannot more freely command in his own house than he may do in his inne. And at parting, if he give some few pence to the chamberlain and ostler, they wish him a happy journey'.

An early edict produced during the reign of James I laid down specific rules and regulations concerning the general administration and running of inns, to be

The Old Welsh Harp at Waltham Abbey, Essex. The adjoining house was originally a brew-house and the pub probably takes its name from the harp-shaped reservoir which is in the vicinity.

The Laurel Inn is at Robin Hood's Bay on the Yorkshire coast.

observed by both innkeepers and guests alike. Solemnly it quoted various scriptural references that pertained to inns and ended by adjuring the guest to *'Eat and drinke for necessity and strength, and not for lust'*.

In 1606 a new act was passed, placing further restrictions upon the buying and selling of ale and beer. The Repression of Drunkenness Act replaced earlier laws and felt that it needed to be explicit by saying: *'The ancient and principal true use of innes and victuallinge houses was for the receipte, relief and lodginge of wayfaring people travelling from place to place'*.

A 'wayfaring' person later became known as the 'bona fide' traveller and was permitted to obtain drinks at hours that were normally forbidden to local residents. This often resulted in hilariously amusing mass exoduses from one town to another so that the residents from one town could be found drinking in the neighbouring town, thus evading the licensing laws.

Although parliamentary acts generally tend to be unpopular when they are designed to curb social and drinking activities and it is possible that the dour monarch disapproved of drink as much as he disliked tobacco, the law did provide certain safeguards that were in the traveller's favour. Ale-house keepers were required to keep 'one or more spare beds' for the lodging of strangers and a landlord who refused to furnish a room without good cause could be compelled to accept the guest, with the help of the local constable. Constables were authorised to force admittance into any inn.

The White Horse, Chilgrove,
Sussex.

The Montagu Arms, Beaulieu,
Hants., shows the arms of the
Montagu family.

It was only the tavern keepers who were exempt from this law and were forbidden to provide lodgings. One unfortunate publican in Hitchin was charged with the offence of *'exposing bread and beer as well for men and horses'*. (Hertfordshire County Records, Vol I: page 30). The Stuarts were, in time, to pass many more acts, none of which were popular with the brewers who had to face increased taxation. Charles I granted a special charter to the citizens of London enabling them to construct signs for the purpose of *'the better finding out such citizen's dwellings'* and also served as address locaters long before the idea of street numbering was thought of. As early as 1393 Richard II had ordered publicans to display signs.

One of the most elaborate and unusual inn signs ever to be built, either then or today, was at Scole in Norfolk and belonged to the **White Hart Inn.** It consisted of a huge carved archway, decorated with an array of Biblical and legendary characters and animals. An engraving of this sign can be seen at the Norwich Central Library. The actual sign was destroyed almost two hundred years ago.

Because so many inns and taverns were situated close to churches, and in some cases actually within churchyards, church wardens and choirboys were frequently seen slipping into the inn whilst the sermon was being preached. This was confirmed by Defoe in the lines:

'Wherever God erects a House of Prayer,
The Devil's sure to build a chapel there,
And 'twill be found upon examination,
The latter has the larger congregation'.

The George, Crawley, Sussex. Situated on the Brighton road, this former medieval dwelling is believed to have become an inn in 1615. It was a popular stage-coach halt and the distinctive gallows sign has been a feature of the inn for well over two hundred and fifty years.

The Prince of Wales, Ledbury, Herefs., in the delightful cobbled Church Lane is one of many beautiful timbered buildings.

It was during the 17th century that we see
the beginning of many of today's leading
brewing companies. Most larger towns had
their own breweries and it is interesting to
note that during Cromwell's short austere
regime he was nicknamed 'The Brewer',
after his mother who had been a brewster in
Huntingdon. It is believed that he first
plotted to overthrow the King at the **Bear**
in Cambridge.

Truman's had been established since 1666.
John Courage began in Southwark in 1787 by
purchasing the Horsely Down brewery;
Southwark ale was known during the 14th
century. Ralph Thrale also had a brewery there
on the site of the former Globe Theatre. This
was later bought by Robert Barclay and
John Perkins and subsequently became part
of the Courage group.

The history of brewers tends to be obscured by
the fact that businesses changed hands and
names were frequently altered. The subject is
worthy of further investigation. Simond's of
Reading and George's of Bristol were taken
over by Courage in 1785 and 1788. Samuel
Whitbread had established his brewery in
London's Chiswell Street and Watney's were
brewing at Wimbledon. Other names rooted in
the 17th and 18th centuries included Allsopp,
Combe, Charrington, Bass, Worthington,
Tetley and Guinness.

The streets of 17th century London must have
created quite a visual impact on any visitor,
who, for the first time, saw a multitude of
elaborate towering signs. Thomas Heywood,
author of the amusing *Roxburghe Ballads*
parodied the names and the types of individuals
who frequented the various taverns:

The King's Head, Lymington, Hants., stands in a charming Georgian cobbled street.

The George, Stamford, Lincs. This well-known hotel has the largest surviving gallows sign.

'The Gentrie went to the King's Head,
The Nobles unto the Crowne,
The Knights went unto the Golden Fleece,
And the Ploughmen to the Clowne.
The Clergie will dine at the Miter,
The Vintners at the Three Tuns,
The Userers to the Devil will goe,
And the Fryers to the Nunnes.
The Cheter will dine at the Checker,
The Picke-pockets in a blind alehouse,
Til on they tride then up Holborne they ride,
And they there end up at the Gallowes'.

The great London fire of 1666 wiped out most of the street signs, as well as entirely destroying a large part of the city. In 1667 an act was passed which prohibited large overhanging street signs. By the turn of the century, this statute had been disregarded and many unwieldy signs re-appeared in the London streets. It was not until four people were killed in a street tragedy in 1718 that further action was taken. The accident occurred in Bride Street when a large overhead sign crashed down, bringing with it the entire front of a shop. There were still those willing to flout the law and as late as 1787, the biographer of Joseph Hanway wrote: *'How comfortless must be the sensations of an elderly female stopped in the street on a windy day under a large old sign loaded with lead and iron in full swing over her head, and perhaps a torrent of dirty water falling near from a projecting spout, ornamented with the mouth and teeth of a dragon. These dangers and distresses are now at an end; and we may think of them as the sailor does of a storm that has subsided . . .'*

In 1711 Joseph Addison, co-founder of the

The Rising Sun, Lynmouth, Devon, forms part of a lovely terrace of historic thatched cottages.

Journey's End Inn, Ringmore, Devon, claims to date from the 12th century.

The New Inn, Winchelsea, Sussex, forms part of an attractive Regency terrace.

Spectator had observed: *'Our streets are filled with Blue Boars, Black Swans and Red Lions, not to mention Flying Pigs and Hogs in Armour, with many other creatures more extraordinary than any in the deserts of Africa . . . One famous sign, hanging outside a public house in Drury Lane, was of so striking a nature that every day crowds of country people could be seen assembled there, vacantly staring at it for hours. It consisted of a full-length picture of Shakespeare . . . suspended in an elaborate carved and gilded frame from some rich ironwork'.* That particular sign remained until 1775 and could be seen after in a pawnbroker's shop window, until it rotted away.

Much has been written about the 'Gin Era' between 1720 and 1750, when cheap gin was generally available. This was attributed to the fact that between 1740 and 1742 there were twice as many burials as baptisms. *'Drunk for 1d, dead drunk for 2d, straw for nothing'* so a popular saying went. Hogarth's propagandist cartoons, *Gin Lane* and the *Four Stages of Cruelty* depicted drunken debauchery of the most evil kind, whereas the contrasting peace and tranquillity of *Beer Street* is distinctly noticeable.

One of the greatest pub-crawlers of the time was the burly lexicographer and prominent literary figure, Dr. Samuel Johnson. The faithful biographer, Boswell, recorded his friend as saying: *'There is nothing which has yet been contrived by man, by which so much happiness is produced as by a good tavern or inn'.*

Johnson spent many an hour in various London pubs and the **Cheshire Cheese** in Johnson Court, today exhibits his notorious chair. Perhaps, above all other taverns, it is the

The Red Lion, Northleach, Glos.,
in an historic old wool town set
in the Cotswolds.

Bel & the Dragon, Cookham,
Berks, recalls an old legend.

35

Mitre in Fleet Street which we mostly associate with Johnson, although this should not be confused with the **Mitre** that Shakespeare knew.

The scholarly Mrs. Thrale, daughter-in-law to the brewer, was a close friend of Johnson's and it is probable that he would have been acquainted with the processes of brewing after visiting the Southwark brewery.

Ownership of many of the taverns and pubs was already in the hands of several of the breweries. An advertisement in the *Daily Courant* emphasised the advantages of free houses over those that were tied:
'A handsome corner public house, in New Belton Street, St. Giles' . . . just empty, well situated and free from bondage of any particular brewer'.

During the years 1751-53 further laws were enacted, this time to prevent distillers from selling or retailing spirits in unlicensed premises. Annual licenses were made statutory and anyone who wished to apply for a license for the first time was required to produce character certificates from clergymen.

The 1751 act preambled:
'Whereas the immoderate drinking of distilled spiritous liquors by persons of the meanest and lowest sort, hath of late years increased, to the great detriment of the health and morals of the common people . . .'

The coaching inns played an essential part in 18th century travel and, generally speaking, the service that they provided was good.

Regular scheduled coach services stopped at selected inns along the route where the horses would be changed and passengers could rest

The Mermaid Inn, Rye, Sussex. This well preserved inn was a notorious haunt of smugglers during the 18th century, and was awarded the Queen's Award to Industry in 1973, in recognition of its achievements in attracting overseas visitors.

Bobby's, Edinburgh.

and take refreshments. Most important towns were well served, with several coaches arriving and leaving every day. Bath, the fashionable society resort presided over by Beau Nash was particularly well provided with coaches.

Travellers were still not infrequently stopped and robbed during a journey and despite the certain fate that befell a captured highwayman, there were plenty of rogues who anxiously engaged in robbing whoever they chanced to meet. The writings of Horace Walpole and the poem by Alfred Noyes have helped to evoke a romantic glamour around the exploits of highwaymen. There was still a persistent belief that many innkeepers were in league with the villains. In 1876 some workmen who were demolishing an inn near Selby stumbled across the remains of a body with a mail bag, hidden in a secret alcove.

Richard Turpin, alias John Palmer is alleged to have killed his friend Tom King in the yard of the **Red Lion** in Whitechapel High Street, a short while before he was hanged at York. Others met their fate at Tyburn (where London's Marble Arch now stands). It was customary to allow the condemned prisoners to have a drink before being executed and the carts would often stop between the prison and the gallows. Swift wrote:

'As clever Tom Clinch, while the rabble was
bawling,
Rode stately through Holborn to die in his calling,
He stopped at the George for a bottle of sack,
And promised to pay for it – when he came back!'

Throughout the 19th century, acts of parliament affecting licensing, opening hours and other measures aimed at curbing drunkenness considerably changed the role of

The Smith's Arms, Godmanstone, Dorset, is the smallest public house in the United Kingdom, measuring just 10 feet wide and 4 feet high at the eaves. It was personally licensed by Charles II who stopped to have his horse shod. When he demanded a drink, the blacksmith told him that he was not licensed to sell ale. The King immediately granted a license in order to get a drink. The bar, however, is not the smallest to be found in the UK.

The Three Mariners in Scarborough dates back to 1300 and was for many years a favourite haunt of smugglers. The building contains several secret escape passages and although no longer used as a pub, it has been specially preserved as a museum. The bar contains a snug which is a common feature of many of our older pubs. They were intended as intimate, exclusive compartments said to 'protect the social susceptibilities of drinkers'.

the pub. More and more pubs became tied to brewers who claimed that they could build better premises and provide a greater selection of drinks.

During Wellington's time as Prime Minister, *The Beer House Act* came into force, entitling anyone to retail beer in return for an annual fee of two guineas. The result of this was quite phenomenal, with 30,978 new beer houses being opened. Understandably, many publicans objected to the competition and suggested that the nation would derive more by appropriating church property, in preference to property belonging to licensed victuallers. It was argued that the clergy did not attend to the poor whereas the pubs did!

The artistic and literary works of the last century have left a rich variety of pub descriptions but the name that most people associate with pubs, is of course, Dickens. The **Ye Olde King's Head** at Chigwell became the *Maypole* in *Barnaby Rudge*. The **Leather Bottle** at Chobham (Kent) contains several mementos of Dickens and any readers of the *Pickwick Papers* will no doubt remember the *Bull* at Rochester or the *Great White Horse* at Ipswich, where Pickwick mistook a lady's bedroom for his own. There are also a number of Dickensian pubs taking their names from famous characters, such as the old **Our Mutual Friend** in Stevenage which stood close to Knebworth House, where Dickens occasionally visited his friend Bulwer Lytton.

There are numerous other literary associations with various pubs but perhaps one of the most amusing is the **Swan** in Grasmere. Sir Walter Scott was staying with the penurious William Wordsworth, and, preferring the hospitality

The Axe & Compass, Hemingford
Abbots, Hunts.

The Pilot Boat Inn, Bembridge,
Isle of Wight.
This unusual-looking inn was
originally a cottage but it has
subsequently been licensed and
rebuilt to give it a nautical
atmosphere.

The Pike & Eel Inn, near
Needingworth, Hunts.

of the local, used regularly to slip out of the house. One day the two men called at the inn to hire some ponies when the landlord tactlessly remarked that Scott had arrived a little early for his daily tot!

William Makepeace Thackeray couldn't help writing a verse about a particular barmaid to whom he was attracted, named Peggy:

'See her as she moves,
Scarce the ground she touches,
Airy as a fay,
Graceful as a duchess . . .'

The Victorians built hundreds of public houses and although many of them were hardly an architectural asset, there were 118,602 licensed premises in 1869 and almost 50,000 breweries and distilleries. Since then there has been a drastic reduction and today there are just over 73,000 premises in the United Kingdom.

Of the 95 brewers, 7 comprise national companies and there are about 15,000 free houses.

The swing towards temperance at the end of the last century presented a serious threat to the industry and it was partly to offset this that the Brewers' Society was established in 1904. The distillers also formed their own society. New laws concerning Sunday closing came into effect but in Wales, some astute publicans provided their customers with specially made metal flasks which could be concealed beneath clothing. These 'belly cans' made it possible for customers to take drinks home on Sundays.

Several temperance societies were formed, with the support of most of the religious institutions. Young children were

The Sole Bay Inn, Southwold,
Suffolk, is a quayside pub,
overshadowed by a lighthouse.

The Cob Tree, Ightham, Kent.

indoctrinated into signing pledges of abstinence at ages when they would never have even contemplated taking liquor.

Probably the most serious threat to the trade came in 1915 when the *Defence of the Realm Act* nationalised 321 licensed premises in the Carlisle, Gretna and Cromarty areas which also included two breweries. These areas were important war production zones and it was felt that essential work was being hampered by excessive drinking. Since 1970, they have been returned to private ownership.

In 1923 drinking was made illegal for those under the age of 18. Throughout the 20's and 30's various attempts to introduce prohibition failed, despite considerable pressure from a number of distinguished people.

The pub has managed to survive in a world of radical change even although television and other forms of relaxation have produced competition. Over a period of hundreds of years, the pub has attained stature and maturity and today has finally become respected and appreciated as an important community social centre.

The George, Chepstow, Mon.,
stands beside the old town gate.

The Fox and Hounds, Barley, Herts.

Pub Signs

In bygone days the pictorial sign was used as a means of identification which could be recognised by even the most ignorant. Long before street naming and numbering became fashionable, the sign was an essential means of locating addresses. Some of the earliest signs were used by the Romans. A chequered sign has been found in the ruins of Pompeii and the ale stake and evergreen is one of the earliest signs used to denote an inn.

Later, other objects, some of them associated with brewing, became synonymous with ale-houses and taverns. Because the Church was closely tied to many of the early inns, the signs appropriately showed a religious influence of apostles, saints and crusades. Other signs reflected royal and heraldic influences.

A certain amount of prestige was attached to establishments which could display the most original and colourful signs and in many instances the work was done by accomplished artists of the day. The less inspired signmaker could always revert to one of the many hackneyed rhymes in an effort to tempt custom:

'If you go by and thirsty be,
The fault's on you and not on me.
Fixed here I am, and hinder none,
So refresh, and pay, and travel on.'

and for the fatigued coach traveller or rider:–

'In this tavern you may find
Everything to suit your mind,
Good wine, good fish, and flesh in courses
Coaches, chaises, harness, horses'.

Often a pub name can mean a lot more than it superficially suggests. Usually the names have

Religious Signs

been carefully chosen, representing a rich accumulation of local folklore and history. Sign spotters can find an extensive variety of artistically attractive notices, although there are also, of course, a few shoddy and inferior ones to be seen.

Religious Signs

Some of the earliest religious signs are strongly linked with the Crusades. The **Ye Olde Trip to Jerusalem** at Nottingham is an obvious example, as are names like the **Turk's** or **Saracen's Head.** There is a well known **Saracen's Head** at Ware, in Hertfordshire.

Devils and demons make interesting subjects. There used to be a well known **Devil** near St. Dunstan's Church, London and the sign depicted St. Dunstan pulling the devil by his nose. Perhaps one of the most enigmatic subjects are our first parents, Adam and Eve, who can leave the artist with a great deal of scope for his imagination. The inevitable happened in one village where the unfortunate artist had the sign returned to him with instructions to equip the duo with fig leaves. Later still, the sign was again returned following complaints about the artist's interpretation of the serpent.

The **Lion & Lamb** depicts the sacrificial Christ and Peter likened 'Satan unto a lion'. **Cross Keys** are associated with the apostle Peter. The **Goat & Compasses** is believed by many to be a corruption of a Puritan motto 'God

encompasses us'. Most *New Inn* signs are in fact
old establishments and can be classified as
religious in origin, taking their names from the
days when inns were administered by
monasteries. The **New Inn** of Gloucester is a
good example of a pilgrims' hostelry. The
Mitre is a well known ecclesiastical symbol and
several pubs bearing the name were known to
Shakespeare, Jonson and Johnson. Some
religious signs disappeared after the
Reformation and it is said that 'papistical'
signs such as the **Nuns** were changed to **Angels.**
Some Angel signs depict Michael the Archangel
carrying a sword and shield.

Various saints appear on signs but one of the
most common is England's patron saint,
George, killing the dragon. Both characters
may also appear on boards separately and a
number of George's were changed to represent
reigning monarchs. Various **Bell** and **Anchor**
compositions are used. Paul described hope as
the 'anchor of the soul', hence the variation
Hope and Anchor.

Heraldic and Emblematic Signs

A wide selection of differing signs within this
grouping represent the monarchy and
aristocracy. During the Middle Ages it was
customary for the houses of the nobility to be
used as hostelries, when the families were
absent. The houses displayed the family's
heraldic coats of arms. Many a shrewd
innkeeper showed his loyalty by adopting the

heraldic device of a neighbouring noble or of the monarch. These signs must have changed as frequently as heads rolled and when Richard III was killed many of the Plantagenet **White Boars** were subsequently painted blue to represent the Earl of Oxford who was instrumental in placing Henry Tudor on the throne. Shortly before being killed, Richard spent his last night in the **White Boar** at Leicester.

Signs depicting animals and birds are also often associated with noble families. The **Greyhound** is the emblem of the Tudors, although it may since have become more associated with sport. The **Talbot,** an extinct breed of dog, represents the Earls of Shrewsbury. A more vulgar form has been passed down as the **Spotted Dog.** Swans appear in the arms of the Buckinghams. The **Swan** at Denham, Bucks shows an example of a chained swan.

One of the Warwicks is reputed to have fought with a bear, a symbol which the family later adopted. This may also appear as a sign which formerly was used to advertise bear baiting. The Stanleys, Earls of Derby, have adopted an unusual emblem, the **Eagle and Child,** and are said to have taken it from the Latham family of Lancashire, to whom Sir John Stanley was related by marriage. One of the Lathams was rumoured to have adopted a child found in an eagle's nest in Ireland. There are numerous rose signs representing the houses of York and Lancaster. The **Rose Revived** and the **Rose & Crown** commemorate the end of the wars between the two houses. Property which stood on ground once owned by the sovereign was often given the name **Crown. Three**

Heraldic and Emblematic Signs.

Crowns refers to the Magi – the three Kings of Orient. The **Crown & Cushion** at Minley, Hampshire has a yew tree, trimmed to the shape of a crown resting on a cushion to commemorate the arrest of Colonel Blood at the inn.

Lions are also popular symbols and appear as **Red Lions, Golden Lions, Black Lions, White Lions** and occasionally, **Blue Lions.** The **Red Lion** represented John of Gaunt and is also found in the arms of Scotland. **Golden Lions** are emblems of England. **White Lions** belong to the Dukes of Norfolk.

Tabards are short sleeved heraldic tunics, blazoned with the arms of the sovereign. Our illustration shows an unusual and realistic carved sign of the **Tabard.**

When Charles II escaped following the Battle of Worcester, he is said to have hidden in an oak tree at Boscobel, hence the popularity of the **Royal Oak** sign.

Many of our monarchs appear on signs, either above the sovereign's name or as the **King's** or **Queen's Head.** Occasionally a playing card representation is used.

The **White Hart,** depicting a pure white stag wearing a gold collar and chain can be traced back to the story told by Pliny in which Alexander the Great captured a stag, placing a gold collar around its neck. Richard II adopted the emblem. Throughout the country there are numerous signs depicting the coats of arms of local noble families. The **Fleur De Lys** obviously relates to the Conquest and shows a Norman warrior.

50

Travel Signs

Transport through the ages is a subject well covered by inn signs. Ever since the Romans set up shop here, roadside inns have provided refreshments and rest for travellers. Our signs depict various travel scenes, ranging from the primitive to the highly sophisticated modes of transport. The **Pilgrim** and the **Traveller's Rest** are often seen. This sign shows a Roman Centurion. There is an unusual sign in Mayfair, London showing a foot-post man delivering mail. The pub is called **I am the only Running Footman.** The stage coach features on many signs and names like the **Coach and Horses,** the **Dairy Maid** and the **Toll House** are quite common. A famous coach, the **Gloucester Flying Machine** can be seen at Brockworth, Gloucestershire. The **Horse and Groom** is another popular sign, and was used to advertise stabling facilities. Horseshoes and blacksmiths were also used for this purpose.

The industrial revolution saw the demise of horse travel and the gradual introduction of steam railways. The **Railway King** at York shows the portrait of George Hudson, a pioneer builder. Many of the great railway hotels and inns no longer survive and some of the existing places have changed their names. It is, however, still possible to find such names as **Great Northern, Great Western, North British, Iron Horse, Puffing Billy, Rocket, Deltic** and the **Railway Tavern.** A model of Stephenson's *Rocket* is affixed to the structure of the **Iron Horse** at Newton Aycliffe, Co. Durham.

Nautical scenes have fared better and it is easy enough to find a variety of ships, either old or new. The **Anchor** is sometimes used to denote a religious meaning but there are plenty of

Sporting Signs

Jolly Sailors, Admirals and **Ships.** Battles and events are also popular, with names like the **Admiral Benbow** and **Trafalgar Tavern.**

Names like the **Airman** can be found in the vicinity of several airports. At Feltham, Middlesex, a sign shows an airman standing in the foreground with a Red Arrows' display in the sky. In Hatfield, Hertfordshire, near where De Haviland's developed the Comet stands a pub of the same name. Just outside Gloucester stands a pub which bears the name the **Jet and Whittle** alluding to the nearby factory whence the first jet engine flight took place in 1941.

A pub in Hastings, instead of showing the Iron Duke, displays **Wellington** bombers.

Cars have not been excluded – the **Silver Ghost** at Alvaston, Derby shows a Rolls-Royce on one side and on the reverse the more usual interpretation. The **Flying Lady** at Hungerford, Berkshire also shows a Rolls-Royce car.

Sporting Signs

Most sporting activities have appeared on signs and their meanings are self explanatory. Cricketers revere the **Bat and Ball** in Hambledon, Berkshire, which celebrates the 18th century captain, John Nyren. One side of the sign shows his portrait whilst the other depicts a game on the green. Nottingham's Trent Bridge ground has the **Test Match** and Lord's has its **Tavern.** W. G. Grace and F. R. Spofforth share the sign at the **Yorker** in

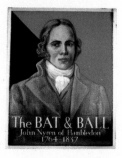

The BAT & BALL
John Nyren of Hambledon
1764–1837

London's Piccadilly. The **Cricketers** at Hebing End, Hertfordshire shows 18th century period costumes and bats. A sign at Newbury, Berkshire is a pun, showing a young girl leaping over the wicket with the lettering **The Maiden Over.**

Some of the football clubs have their own pubs like Arsenal whose supporters can drink at the **Gunners**, Finsbury Park. Golfers are not as well represented although places named after famous holes can sometimes be seen. ·

Anglers can drink at the **Pike and Eel,** Needingworth, Huntingdonshire. Isaac Walton is celebrated at the **Compleat Angler** at Marlow, Buckinghamshire and the **Isaac Walton** at Brimsdown, Middlesex.

Horse Racing has always been a popular subject and names like the **Horse & Groom** or **Horseshoes** can refer to either coaching inns or racing establishments. The **Derby Arms** at East Sheen, Surrey shows Sansovino winning at Epsom in 1924. A St. Leger winner, **Charles XII** is shown along with the 1813 **Altisidora.** The name **Arkle** has become immortal, as has the **Master Robert** who, as a racehorse developed bad legs and was relegated to pulling a milk cart and yet went on to win the Grand National.

Blood sports have always been common. The **Fighting Cocks** at St. Albans reminds us of the now illegal sport of cock-fighting. Other inns have had a tradition for bear-baiting. The **Cat and Custard Pot** is an unusual sign at Shipton Moyne, Wiltshire. On one side can be seen a cat, licking a bowl but the reverse side shows the literary character Jorrocks at a hunt meeting. The crafty fox turns up on a number of signs but perhaps the most extraordinary

The Kill on the Cat & Custard Pot Day

Signs Depicting People

Fox and Hounds is the old gallows sign at Barley, Hertfordshire which completely spans the road. It is said that the name originated after a fox took refuge in a kennel at the back of the inn. Unfortunately, in 1950 the inn was destroyed by fire but the preserved sign was transferred to another pub just a few yards up the road. Hawking and falconry are often shown. Shakespeare knew the **Falcon** at Stratford-upon-Avon. Several monarchs, including Elizabeth I have used the bird as a heraldic symbol.

Signs Depicting People

All kinds of people, whether real life, imaginary or legendary can be seen looking down from their lofty pub signs. Politicians, men of war, royalty, inventive geniuses, noblemen, artists, writers, fictional and folk-lore characters have all been used.

Green Men are traditionally popular inn signs and another green man who allegedly robbed the rich to help the poor called **Robin Hood** is also frequently seen.

Heroic deeds can assure lasting fame and there is certainly no shortage of such people as **Wellington, Nelson, Marquis of Granby, Duke of York** and **Sir Francis Drake.** Politicians and statesmen such as **Oliver Cromwell, Palmerston, Pitt, Gladstone, John F. Kennedy, Churchill, Peel, Disraeli, Lloyd George** and **Clement Attlee.** When Attlee's portrait sign was unveiled for

Signs Depicting People

the pub's opening in Fulham, attended by his son, it was discovered that the artist had depicted the former prime minister wearing a red tie. The sign had to be removed and the colour of the tie changed because, as it was pointed out, he never ever wore a red tie!

Great men like **Wren, Brunel, Cook, Shakespeare** and **Dickens** have all been captured by the signpainter's brush. We also find famous women like **Florence Nightingale, Amy Johnson, Jenny Lind, Nell Gwynne, Emma Hamilton, Nellie Dean, Eliza Doolittle** and the unfortunate **Silent Woman,** showing a headless female. Perhaps the artist decided to make amends when he painted the **Nag's Head** which was not the usual horse portrait.

Regimental orders are found, particularly close to barracks and the signs often depict a regiment's most famous battle scene. Pubs have not been without their share of villainy so it is fitting that we should also come across rogues like **Claude Duval,** the **Wicked Lady,** the **Highwayman** and scenes depicting punishments such as the **Stocks or Gibbet.**

Doctor William Harvey who discovered the principal of blood circulation is shown on a distinctive sign at the **William Harvey** near Ashford, Kent. The pub stands on the former site of the Harvey Cottages at Willesborough and the sign is unusual in that it uses a contemporary engraving of the doctor. One of the most quaint and infrequent signs that we see nowadays is the **Five Alls** showing five representations:– 'I Pray for All', 'I Fight for All', 'I Rule for All', 'I Plead for All', and 'I Work for All'. Other variations of this theme are known to exist.

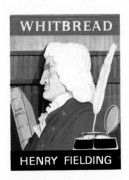

Legendary characters which include **Dick**

Whittington, the **Pied Piper,** the **Babes in the Wood, Tom Thumb, Robinson Crusoe, Jack and Jill** and **Mother Hubbard** seem to be very popular. The local conundrum about the polygamous man and his seven wives is depicted on a sign at St. Ives, Huntingdon:

'As I was going to St. Ives
I met a man with seven wives,
Each wife with seven sacks
Each sack with seven cats . . .'

One of Hogarth's original signs has often been imitated. It is called a **Load of Mischief** and depicts a man carrying on his shoulders, fastened by a chain, his drunken wife, a monkey and a magpie. Another of his signs is slightly more distasteful, showing John the Baptist's head on a charger and entitled **Good Eating**.

Trade Signs

It used to be common practice for all businesses to display descriptive trade signs, but nowadays, with the exception of barbers, chemists and possibly pawnbrokers, it is only the brewing industry which has kept the tradition alive. Varying trades can be found on our pub signs and some of them would indicate an historical association. The smallest pub in Britain, the **Smith's Arms,** Godmanstone, Dorset was a blacksmith's forge in Charles II's day. He stopped there to have his horse shod and when told he couldn't buy

a drink he immediately granted a license and the pub was named the **Smith's Arms**.

Places called the **Farrier's Arms** or the **Three Horseshoes** could well have formerly housed a forge.

The **Wheatsheaf** has links with the Earls of Exeter but is usually associated with baking. Traditional farming implements such as the **Plough**, the **Reaper** and the **Haycart** are frequently seen, as are names like the **Jolly Farmer, Poulterer's Arms, Gardener's Arms** and **Ploughboy**.

Apart from the obvious Biblical associations, **Noah's Ark** has served as the crest of the London Company of Shipwrights. The **Lamb** represented the tailoring trade and the **Lamb & Flag** has been derived from the Merchant Tailors' Company.

The **Ye Olde Pump House** of Hastings is so named because at one time it was the only place where people could draw fresh water in the town. The bar contains an interesting collection of curios and bric-a-brac.

Watermen have the **Watermen's Arms** and in Anglesey, in the town of Llangefni there is a pub in the market square called the **Market Vaults**.

The **Fleece** or **Woolpack** have been used as emblems for the wool trade since the 14th century.

London's Fetter Lane has the **Printer's Devil**, a modern pub rebuilt after the war and containing an interesting collection of printing ephemera. It is hardly surprising to find several signs directly relating to the brewing trade. Tuns are used as the arms of the ancient Company of Vintners and there are plenty of

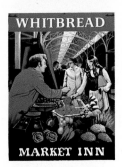

Animal Signs

the following names to be found: **Three Tuns, Hoop & Grapes, Vineyard, Bunch of Grapes, Hop Pole,** and the **Barley Mow,** a traditional countryside sign. **Health to the Barley Mow** is a replica of one painted by Hogarth, showing farmworkers celebrating after a successful harvest.

When new public houses are opened, members of the public are often invited to participate in submitting suggestions for names. The **William Cookworthy** at St. Austell, Cornwall was a popular choice, honouring a notable character who was once associated with the local china clay industry.

Animal Signs

Several of the animals that turn up on signs appear as family crests or coats of arms. Sports and hunting pastimes account for many animals like dogs, hares, rabbits, foxes, stags, falcons, eagles and hawks.

Horses have always been popular symbols, particularly **White Horses** which are sometimes associated with the Hanoverian coat of arms. Around Wiltshire and the West Country, a number of **White Horse** signs relate to the chalk figures cut into the downs.

Various birds such as swans, ducks, magpies, doves, pelicans and cocks are fairly common. At Stonham, Suffolk there is an unusual gallows sign at the **Magpie** which spans the road.

Unusual Signs

Various fishes and sea creatures abound, particularly around the coastal towns and villages.

Cats have always been popular, whether they be the pantomime **Puss in Boots, Cheshire Cat, Mad Cat, Rampant Cat** or the musical **Cat & Fiddle.**

Humorous animals such as the **Snooty Fox, Whistling Duck, Dun Cow** and others can usually arouse a smile. The **Pig & Whistle** is an old name thought to be a corruption of Peg and Wassail, a phrase associated with the custom of drinking to pegs.

The village of Lanivet, Cornwall has a rare animal sign – a **Panda.** One of the village's local industries used to be the growing of bamboos which were used to feed the late Chi Chi of London Zoo.

The faithfulness of a dog is remembered in Edinburgh, the home of the famous Greyfriars Bobby who kept vigil for his departed master. A nearby pub has been named **Bobby's.**

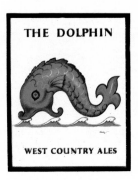

Unusual Signs

This last category includes a few of the many unusual and striking pub signs that are either amusing or of a serious nature.

A sign in Chingford shows a side of beef being knighted by King James I and is called the **Sir Loin.** The **World Turned Upside Down,** near Reading shows a donkey sitting in a cart being pulled by a man, a pig killing a butcher,

a bear with a dancing man, a rat chasing a cat and dogs ridden by foxes chasing a man! Knaresborough has the **End of the World**.

The **Hole in the Wall** is an amusing name which is said to have originated from a hole in the wall of a debtor's prison, through which the inmates received gifts. The Highwayman Claude Duval was captured at a pub of the same name in London. The sign in the illustration is a modern interpretation.

The **Snow Drop Inn** of Lewes, Sussex sounds a pretty enough name but it is not named after the flower. An avalanche killed several people in the area during the 19th century.

Another Sussex pub, the **Runt-in-Tun** has just been reopened after a number of years of closure. The ancient name really means pig in the barrel.

The **Nut Shell,** so appropriately named, at Bury St. Edmunds has the smallest bar, measuring a mere fifteen feet.

Dirty Dick's in Bishopsgate, London is named after an old hermit. Architecturally, one of the most exciting modern pubs is an extraordinary 70 foot high fairy-tale castle at Dunstable called the **Windsock,** in honour of the local gliding club.

The **Crooked Billet** sign is made out of wood and contains an unusual inscription which has been copied from the fireplace of the inn.

The **Four Counties** Inn happens to stand on No Man's Heath where the counties of Staffordshire, Derbyshire, Warwickshire and Leicestershire come together. Some pubs get their names by accident. An amusing example of this can be seen in the former **Royal Oak** at Westbury-on-Trym, near

Unusual Signs

Bristol. Several years ago the sign was removed and the villagers hung a mouse in its place. The house became known unofficially as the **Mouse** and eventually the owners were obliged to change the name officially.

Young's, the London brewers once named a pub after one of their employees. On the ancient highway, Watling Street, at Rainham Mark, Kent, stands the **Belisha Beacon Inn,** honouring a former Secretary of State and ardent road safety supporter, Leslie Hore-Belisha. When opened in 1938 the inn was the first of its kind to be named in honour of a living notability.

The former **Red Lion** near Iver, Bucks, was renamed the **Gurkha** as a tribute to the soldiers who have maintained a close link with Britain for over 170 years.

The uncoveted honour of unfriendliest pub must go to a pub in Glencoe, Scotland which exhibited a sign for a number of years – **No Campbells.**

Bibliography

There are a number of excellent reference
books providing further information on the
subject of pubs and pub signs. They include:

Trade Signs and their Origins. C. A. Meadows.
Routledge & Kegan Paul. 1957.

Inns, Ales & Drinking Customs of Olde England.
F. W. Hackwood. T. Fisher Unwin. 1909.

Elizabethan Life in Town & Country.
M. St. Clare Byrne. Methuen. 1925.

Chaucer and his England. G. G. Coulton.
Methuen. 1908.

English Social History. Trevelyan. Longman.
1958.

Travel in the 17th Century. J. Parkes. Oxford
University Press. 1933.

History of English Ale and Beer. C. A.
Monckton. Longman. 1966.

Johnson's England. Vols. 1 & 2. Edited by
A. S. Turberville. Clarendon Press. 1933.

Shakespeare's England. Vols. 1 & 2. Clarendon
Press. 1916.

The English Inn. D. Batchelor. Batsford. 1963.

Old Inns of England. W. Gaunt. Batsford.
1958.

Egon Ronay's Pub Guide. The Gas Council/
Hutchinson. 1969.

Inn Signs: Their History and Meaning.
The Brewers' Society. 1969.

Discovering Inn Signs. Cadbury Lamb and
Gordon Wright. Shire Publications. 1968.

Pub Index